# Praying
# the
# Daily
# Gospels

# Praying the Daily Gospels

## A Guide to Meditation

PHILIP A. St. ROMAIN

AVE MARIA PRESS Notre Dame, Indiana

© 1984 by Ave Maria Press

Library of Congress Catalog Card Number: 84-71186

International Standard Book Number: 0-87793-314-6

*Cover and text design:* Elizabeth French

Printed and bound in the United States of America.

# Contents

# Acknowledgments

I do not know Father Henri Nouwen personally, but I am deeply indebted to him for an article he wrote in *America* several years ago, suggesting that the weekday liturgical scriptures provide a wonderful source of material for prayerful meditation. Father Nouwen's suggestion has proven to be true in my own life, and I hope this guide enables others also to experience the richness of the liturgical year.

Many thanks to Father Dan Drinan, Sister Lydia Champagne, Father John Edmunds, and other former colleagues from my days at the Louisiana State University Catholic Student Center, where we all learned the meaning of prayer.

Christ the Servant Cenacle, St. George's and St. Patrick's Parishes helped pilot the Lenten section of this work and provided valuable feedback concerning the content and organization.

No married man with two young daughters can find the time to write and think without the support of an extremely understanding wife. Thanks, Lisa! You helped to make this possible.

# Introduction

Prayer is a hunger experienced by millions of people today. Numerous faith renewal movements sweeping through the church in recent years have deepened in many people an awareness of Jesus Christ as personal Lord and Savior. People are discovering anew a love for the word of God in scripture, striving enthusiastically to understand what is there and to prayerfully reflect on what it calls them to become.

Learning to pray with scripture does not come easily, however. Always there are the distractions we bring to prayer, in addition to the ongoing struggle to find a quiet time to be alone with God. Once settled, there is then the task of identifying a scripture to reflect upon — not always as easy a matter as it might sound. For me and for many with whom I have shared concerning praying with scripture, a variety of approaches is usually adopted.

I have gone through periods when I moved systematically through a section of the Bible, selecting a few verses as food for meditation for each prayer session. This worked well, except for the days when I wound up with a genealogy, or a salutation, or something else that didn't seem to help me lift my mind and heart to God as I had hoped. Another approach involves "cracking" the Bible open, selecting a passage from one of the pages in view. This has proven to be a powerful experience at times — almost like confronting an oracle, but at other times it has produced the same

kinds of dry materials that the systematic process
did. Bible cracking also evoked in me a kind of
superstition about the word of God, as though there
were something extraordinarily significant on the
pages I had opened to. Neither approach provided
lasting satisfaction.

The answer to my struggle to find scriptures to
pray with came through several spiritual writers,
most notably Henri Nouwen, who suggested using
the scripture passages for the church's liturgy of the
day. I began accepting the daily liturgical scriptures for prayerful consideration as I would have
from a director on a retreat, but soon discovered
that the two passages provided more than I could
digest in my few minutes of solitude. A choice
therefore had to be made: Was I to pray with the
first reading, or with the gospel? I chose the gospel,
of course, since in the gospels we encounter Jesus in
a very special way. The gospels present us with the
church's faith-filled memories of the life and
teachings of Jesus. That is what I needed to encounter in prayer.

Praying with the gospel passage from the
liturgy of the day has been a rewarding experience
for me during the past few years. I have found that
this allowed for a fairly comprehensive covering of
all four gospels in a year's time while deeply
enriching my experience of the Mass on the days I
attended. On days when I could not go to Mass,
praying with the church's selections gave me a sense
of being more in tune with the rhythms and
movements developed through the seasons of the
liturgical year. This has been a powerful experience

for me and that is why I recommend it whole-heartedly.

It is important here to point out the difference between praying with scripture and studying scripture. The study of scripture is an important complement to prayer, informing the mind concerning the contexts and meanings that both limit and illuminate the messages of scripture. An overbalance of pious reflection can lead to a narrow perspective on scripture; conversely, too much exegetical reflection can lead one to approach scripture in an analytical frame of mind rather than in openness to encounter God. This balancing between piety and formal study of scripture is a struggle that any committed Christian must not avoid, for the consequences of neglect either way can have serious detrimental influences on personal growth.

In the pages that follow I hope to stimulate prayer by focusing on the gospel passages for the church's seasonal weekday liturgies. For each day, a short note concerning contextual and theological considerations is provided to help dispose the mind for reflection on the questions and ideas which follow. These reflection stimuli are intended to help the reader internalize the meaning of the gospels and apply its message to the concrete circumstances of life.

I have found that writing in a journal is helpful during prayer, and can provide material to go back to from time to time. With journal, Bible and meditation guide, then, let us join the church in her prayer journey through the year.

# Suggestions for Prayer

**Time:** Set aside at least 15 minutes when you can be alone with minimal disturbance; choose a time when your body and mind are awake; be faithful to this time daily and you will actually find yourself looking forward to it.

**Place:** Choose a place that will allow you quiet and solitude; many people go to the same place day after day, designating their prayer place to be holy ground; others find changing places to be enriching; discover what is right for you.

**Decontaminating:** Begin your prayer time by asking God for the grace to discover his love and will for you; share with God the thoughts and feelings that you bring to prayer; tell God who you are right now mentally and emotionally; perhaps a short period of deep breathing and noting the sounds around you can also help to break distractions.

**Psalm Prayer:** Even though your distractions do not cease (they seldom do), read through the psalm prayer of the day; do not try to analyze it, but if something touches you, spend time with it; if distractions persist, don't worry about it.

**Gospel Meditation:** After reading the psalm and a few moments of quiet, read the gospel passage of the day all the way through; let its impact be with you for a while, but don't force yourself to analyze anything; after a few moments of quiet, read the introductory note, then proceed into the passage again, this time more slowly; note what God is revealing and what this means for you in your life; use reflection guides for stimulation, if needed; write impressions in your journal.

**Petition and Thanksgiving:** Express to God your gratitude and awareness of need, being as specific as possible; ask for the grace for yourself and others to love more deeply; avoid prayer lists and dutiful prayer of petition.

**Contemplation:** If you feel led to quiet adoration, cherish this loving exchange with God; if you are not moved to contemplation, do not bother worrying about it; rejoice when you experience silent adoration, rejoice when you do not.

> If, during prayer, you do nothing but bring your heart from distraction again and again into God's presence, though it went away every time you brought it back, your time would be very well employed.
>
> St. Francis de Sales

# The Season of
## Advent

The season of Advent marks the beginning of the church's liturgical year. During this season, preparation for the coming of the Messiah is stressed through Old Testament prophets and Jesus' fulfillment of the prophecies. We are invited through these readings to better prepare our own hearts for Christ's coming into our lives.

# First Week in Advent

**Monday:** *Ps 122: 1-9*
*Mt 8: 5-11 (Healing a centurion's servant)*

Jesus brings health and wholeness to a gentile. For the early church, this incident was a reminder that the Messiah and the graces he won for us are to be extended to all people and not just converts from Judaism. Jesus wants to come to everyone.

- Let your imagination re-create this gospel scene; you take the place of the centurion. See Jesus walking along the road; watch as he notes your approach and gives you his full attention; note his response to your requests for healing in your own life and with loved ones.

- Make a list in your journal of the people in your life for whom you have been called to be an incarnation of God's grace. How can you be a better channel of grace to each of them?

**Tuesday:** *Ps 72: 1, 7-8, 12-13, 17*
        *Lk 10: 21-24 (Jesus rejoices)*

Jesus had sent his 72 disciples out among the people to announce a forthcoming visitation. When the disciples returned to him they were overjoyed that the people were eager to see Jesus. Jesus' delight shows that the gospel is not meant to be a burdensome task.

- Share with God something that has recently happened in your life which you believe helped you and/or another to grow in some way. Let yourself imagine Jesus expressing delight over this.

- How do you feel about Jesus having come? Do you take the incarnation for granted? What does the incarnation mean to you?

**Wednesday:** *Ps 23: 1-6*
        *Mt 15: 29-37 (Jesus feeds the crowd)*

In this passage and in others where miracles are discussed, it is not as important to focus on the extraordinary deed as on what it means. Bread and fish are symbols of the Eucharist, and this passage points up Jesus' power to nourish us in spirit, mind and body.

- Jesus turned a small offering into a feast. What are some of the talents God has given you that you can offer toward the building of his kingdom? How can you better offer these gifts to God?

**Thursday:** *Ps 118: 1, 8-9, 19-21, 25-27*
        *Mt 7: 21, 24-27 (Build wisely)*

We all build our lives on certain beliefs and principles. Jesus tells us that life will test us in many ways, and that if we have built our lives on foundations other than him, life will destroy us.

- In your journal, make a sketch of yourself using a symbol of a house of some kind. What foundation is holding this house up? What kinds of forces are bearing down on your house at this time in your life, threatening to tear it down?

- Pray for the grace to build your life more firmly on Christ.

**Friday:** *Ps 27: 1, 4, 13-14*
        *Mt 9: 27-31 (Jesus cures two blind men)*

Jesus was very aware of his actions and words being misinterpreted by those who had their own ideas about what the Messiah should be. He did not fit the role of political monarch some wanted, nor was he committed to the cause of Jewish nationalism. He saw himself more as a loving servant, and sought frequently to deflect attention away from himself toward his Father.

- If you could ask and receive from God one gift, what would it be? Hear Jesus ask you, "Are you confident that I can do this for you?"

- Ask for the grace to strengthen your faith in God's providence.

**Saturday:** *Ps 147: 1-6*
*Mt 9: 35-10: 1, 6-8 (Jesus shares his mission with us)*

One of the overwhelming implications of the incarnation is that God became human so that humans might become God. Creator of all, God nonetheless chose to share with us his ministry of building the kingdom. We are co-creators and co-redeemers of the world with God.

• At the sight of human suffering, Jesus was moved to compassion. How do you generally feel when, in your daily experience or through the media, you are exposed to the reality of human suffering?

• How do you feel about the statement, "The reign of God is at hand"? Do you believe it?

# Second Week in Advent

**Monday:** *Ps 85: 9-14*
    *Lk 5: 17-26 (Jesus heals a paralyzed man)*

"Who can forgive sins but God alone?" muttered the scribes and the Pharisees in today's reading. Jesus replied by showing them that the same love which heals the body can also heal a guilt-ridden spirit.

- Do you love your body? Do you believe that your own bodily health is a value important to God? Why? (Why not?) Spend some time thanking God for your health, even if you do not enjoy perfect health.

- Hear Jesus saying, "My friend, your sins are forgiven you." Pray for the grace to believe that you are a forgiven sinner.

**Tuesday:** *Ps 96: 1-3, 10-13*
    *Mt 18: 12-14 (The Good Shepherd)*

God loves individuals. This is a revelation sometimes hard for us to grasp because we think that God must be too busy to love us, what with him having to run the universe and all. Yet Jesus tells us that God's greatest joy comes when an individual decides to break with sin and join his Father's fold.

- With whom do you identify most in today's parable: the stray sheep, the 99 faithful ones, or the shepherd in search of the stray? Why?

21

- How do you usually feel when you hear others sharing their conversion experiences? Do you rejoice with them?

**Wednesday:** *Ps 103: 1-4, 8, 10*
    *Mt 11: 28-30 (The gentle Christ)*

We sometimes hear of people sharing their confusion and struggles over discovering what is God's will for them. Today's reading reminds us that God's will is not meant to be burdensome, but refreshing. God is not a judgmental task-master, but a loving support.

- What does Jesus mean when he says his yoke is easy, his burden light? How do you experience this?

- Spend some time with the words, "Come to me." Let yourself feel God's desire for you to be with him.

**Thursday:** *Ps 145: 1, 9-13*
    *Mt 11: 11-15 (Jesus praises John the Baptist)*

The figure of John the Baptist is one revered by the church. John was apparently one of the greatest of Jewish prophets, and many people believed he was the Messiah. Even after the resurrection, we find people who were his disciples proclaiming the coming of the Messiah. The church came to see John as the forerunner of the Messiah, Jesus Christ, and identified him to be the spirit of Elijah prophesied to usher in the new age.

- The spirit of John the Baptist was a spirit of
  boldness and courage, which Winston Chur-
  chill maintained made all other virtues possible. Are you courageous in standing up for the
  gospel?

- Pray for the grace to let go of fear in your life.

**Friday:** *Ps 1: 1-6*
    *Mt 11: 16-19 (The fickleness of the crowds)*

It is impossible to please everybody, Jesus
learned. There were those who believed that he
was too liberal in his following of the Law, and
they condemned him for it. More than likely
these were the same people who believed that
John was too strict. But Jesus did not cater to
public opinion. He was intent only on doing the
will of his Father.

- How important are the opinions of others as influences upon you? Do you find it easy to go
  against the crowd? When do you usually find
  this necessary?

- How do you feel about people who are noncon-
  formists, but for noble reasons? Why?

**Saturday:** *Ps 80: 2-3, 15-16, 18-19*
    *Mt 17: 10-13 (On John and Elijah)*

The Old Testament prophets wrote a number
of things concerning the origins and times of the
Messiah. They expected that he would be of the
house of David, born in Bethlehem, and be

ushered in by the prophet Elijah, who would "turn the hearts of fathers toward their children and the hearts of children toward their fathers" (Mal 3: 24). Jesus tells his disciples that John the Baptist has fulfilled Elijah's role.

- How do you invite the Messiah to work in your life? What virtues are you cultivating as precursors to his actions within you? Think of a person who plays an important role in your life, but whom you have neglected somewhat lately. Make a resolution to let this person know how much you appreciate him or her.

# Third Week in Advent

**Monday:** *Ps 25: 4-9*
*Mt 21: 23-27 (The authority of Jesus)*

The Jewish religious authorities tried many times to trap Jesus in some kind of philosophical dilemma. In today's reading, we find them baiting Jesus by asking him about the sources of his authority. Recognizing the trap, Jesus exposes their hypocrisy and political fears.

- When was the last time you felt "attacked" because of your religious beliefs? How did you respond?

- What does the word "authority" mean to you? How do you usually feel about authorities?

- Pray for the grace to be more submissive to the authority of Christ.

**Tuesday:** *Ps 34: 2-3, 6-7, 17-19, 23*
*Mt 21: 28-32 (The meaning of obedience)*

Many people rebel against the idea of obedience because they believe it entails mindless submission. In today's parable, however, we learn that those who choose to obey the will of God by living a life of love are exercising human freedom in the best possible manner.

- An old saying has it that the road to hell is paved with good intentions. Do you agree with this point. Why? (Why not?)

- Can you think of something that needs to be done to make your life or your family's life richer, but which you have procrastinated in beginning? Resolve to make a start today.

**Wednesday:** *Ps 85: 9-14*
       *Lk 7: 18-23 (John's disciples seek the*
              *Messiah)*

It is apparent that even John the Baptist was surprised at the kind of Messiah Jesus was turning out to be. Jesus reassured his imprisoned friend that making people whole is more important than political glory.

- Do you often question who Jesus was and what he was about? Do you find such questioning a threat to your faith? Why? (Why not?) How do you feel about the response Jesus gave to John's disciples? How well does his response describe your own lifestyle?

**Thursday:** *Ps 30: 2-6, 11-13*
        *Lk 7: 24-30 (Jesus praises John)*

Many people had gone far out of their way to hear John the Baptist and to be baptized by him. Jesus affirmed their recognition of John's greatness, but challenged them to grow in the Spirit to even greater heights.

**Friday:** *Ps 67: 2-3, 5, 7-8*
      *Jn 5: 33-36 (The testimony of Jesus and*
            *John)*

John the Baptist, our Advent guide, was the one who prepared the people for the works that Jesus was to do among them. In today's reading, Jesus points to these works as evidence that God has sent him.

* Look over the works you have performed during the past two days. To whom do they testify?

* What kinds of charitable works have you been neglecting lately? Make a resolution to begin on at least one of them today.

**December 17:** *Ps 72: 3-4, 7-8, 17*
   *Mt 1: 1-17 (Matthew's genealogy)*

Genealogies are among the most difficult of scriptures to use as grist for prayer. Matthew's genealogy was carefully constructed to trace Jesus' origins back through the line of David, as the prophet Nathan had foreseen. The accuracy of this genealogy is contested by some scripture scholars, but it still points up the very human side of the Messiah.

* Make a diagram sketching your own family tree, over two or three generations if you can.

* Glancing over your family tree, try to recall at least one way in which each individual you've listed has loved you through the years. Give thanks to God for these graces.

**December 18:** *Ps 72: 1, 12-13, 18-19*
   *Mt 1: 18-24 (The angel and Joseph)*

Joseph and Mary were betrothed when Mary became pregnant with Jesus. To Joseph, this indicated that Mary had been unfaithful, so he wanted to break off the relationship. This tradition and the story of the angelic appearance in today's reading give us a clue as to the Messiah's identity: He is a child of the Holy Spirit.

• Looking over the family tree you sketched yesterday, draw lines between yourself and those family members you feel close to. Write in a comment about your relationship with each person next to your lines.

• Draw lines between yourself and those family members you do not feel close to. Write a comment about why you feel distant from each.

• Pray that the Messiah may come to your family this Christmas.


**December 19:** *Ps 71: 3-6, 16-17*
   *Lk 1: 5-25 (The origins of John the Baptist)*

The story of Jesus is inseparable from that of John the Baptist. The two men were related by blood and by the Holy Spirit. The conception of John by the elderly Zechariah and Elizabeth brings to mind the birth of Isaac and the nation of Israel by the aged Abraham and Sarah.

• Do you believe you are too old to change some of your ways?

- Spend some time with the passage, "In these days, the Lord is acting on my behalf." Let these words sink in and believe in them.

- By the way, how well are you handling Christmas preparations this year? Are you getting too caught up in the card-writing, gift-buying spirit?

**December 20:** *Ps 24: 1-6*
        *Lk 1: 26-38 (The Annunciation)*

Mary shall always occupy a unique place in salvation history. It was her acceptance of God's invitation that brought the Messiah into the world. She is a model for all who struggle to give birth to the Messiah in their own lives.

- How do you feel about Mary? What virtues does she model that appeal to you?

- Spend some time with the passage, "Behold the servant of the Lord; let his will be done in my life." Pray that this attitude will take deep root within you.

**December 21:** *Ps 33, 2-3, 11-12, 20-21*
        *Lk 1: 39-45 (The Visitation)*

It is always a sweet moment when we realize that other people understand our struggles and share our pain. Though years apart in age, Mary and Elizabeth shared such a moment when Mary visited her wise cousin. Luke wrote of this time of joy for our edification.

- Think of a joyous statement to share with your family today. Resolve to share this joy.

- As Christmas approaches, charity in giving can fall prey to compulsion and last-minute sprees. How are you managing your shopping this year?

**December 22:** *1 Sm 2: 1, 4-8*
   *Lk 1: 46-56 (Mary's Magnificat)*

The Magnificat is one of the most profound prayers of the Bible, summing up salvation history and important Old Testament revelations about God. Luke has Mary uttering these words because she was the one upon whom God bestowed the responsibility of bearing the Messiah.

- Spend a few moments with each passage, letting the words speak to you and your life situation. Stay with the passages that move you.

- Pray for the grace to praise God.

**December 23:** *Ps 25: 4-5, 8-10, 14*
   *Lk 1: 57-66 (Zechariah names his son)*

Jews believed that a person's name influenced the development of his or her character, and that to know a person's name was to have an entry into his or her soul. The story of the naming of John the Baptist pointed out the influence of God in the life of this last Jewish prophet.

- How did you get your name? What qualities of character does your name suggest to you?

- Look in the mirror sometime today and tell yourself, "God doesn't make junk." Smile at yourself, then, and pray for the grace to love yourself.

- Spend some time with the passage: "The hand of God was (is) upon him (me)."

**December 24:** *Ps 89: 2-5, 27, 29*
         *Lk 1: 67-79 (Zechariah's Canticle)*

Just as he did in Mary's Magnificat, Luke wrote of salvation history in Zechariah's Canticle. This is a prayer used daily in the Liturgy of the Hours, and is an inspiring statement about God's love for us. It is a prayer rich in meaning concerning both John the Baptist and us.

- Read through this passage slowly, spending time with the verses that move you. Write your impressions in your journal.

- Christmas day is tomorrow. Will charity prevail? How will you celebrate the incarnation?

# Christmas
## Season

Christ has come, and the world can never again be the same. During the days that follow, we will be reflecting upon a number of occasions that describe the meaning of the incarnation. We will be invited to continue the journey we began in Advent, only now with a new appreciation of the tremendous grace that has come to us in Jesus Christ.

## December 26: *Ps 31: 3-4, 6-8, 17, 21*
### *Mt 10: 17-22 (St. Stephen's martyrdom)*

Recent studies have shown that the placement of this feast day in the church's liturgical calendar has little to do with its proximity to Christmas. Yet St. Stephen's martyrdom can serve to remind us that crucifixion is the price paid for incarnation. Today's gospel brings this point home, while promising glory for those who, like Stephen, held out until the end.

- In what ways do you die for Christ each day? How do these deaths to self allow the incarnation to happen in your life?

- Do you believe that you, at this point in your life, would be willing to die for your faith? Why? (Why not?)

- Pray for the grace to be willing to suffer for the sake of love.

**December 27:** *Ps 97: 1-2, 5-6, 11-12*
       *Jn 20: 1-8 (St. John, apostle and evangelist)*

In contrast to the martyrdom of the youthful Stephen, John the apostle is said to have lived to be a very old man. He alone out of all the apostles escaped violent martyrdom, showing the early church that it was possible to persevere in charity until a ripe old age — perhaps a more difficult challenge after all. His disciples left us a magnificent gospel, a tribute to the belief he came to as described in today's passage.

• In your imagination, journey with Peter and the beloved disciple to the tomb of Jesus. Note their shortness of breath as they arrive; feel their wonder as they venture inside, only to find the tomb vacated.

• Do you believe that Jesus Christ rose from the dead?

• Pray for the grace to be open to new life.

**December 28:** *Ps 124: 2-5, 7-8*
       *Mt 2: 13-18 (Holy Innocents, martyrs)*

In today's reading we commemorate an event almost too horrible to believe. Tradition has it that Herod the Great, upon hearing of the birth of Jesus, the Messiah-king, was overcome with jealousy and ordered all infant boys in the Bethlehem area slain. This treachery is one of many examples of sin and wickedness history records to help us recognize our need for salvation.

- How do you feel about the torturing of political prisoners and of innocent victims in oppressive regimes? What is your response to this?

- Are you jealous of anyone or any group of people?

- Pray for the grace to be able to accept people just as they are.

**December 29:** *Ps 96: 1-3, 5-6*
*Lk 2: 22-35 (Jesus' consecration)*

Always good Jews, Joseph and Mary were faithful in keeping the Mosaic Law. Their consecration of Jesus was in keeping with a tradition that went back many years. Simeon's words on this occasion describe some of the roles the Messiah is to play.

- What do you hope to accomplish and/or become before you die? What are you doing now to help realize this dream?

- What is it about your work that contributes to the building of God's kingdom on earth?

**December 30:** *Ps 96: 7-10*
*Lk 2: 36-40 (More prophecies about Jesus)*

The religious heroes of all traditions usually come to us replete with mysterious origins and wonderful prophecies; stories about Jesus are no

exception. It is said that Luke gathered much of
the material for his infancy narratives from
Mary, who had treasured the events of that time
in her heart. Today's reading with Anna's prophecy may well be one such event.

• How do you feel about the notion that Jesus
  *grew* in strength, grace and wisdom?

• What are you doing to keep growing in your
  appreciation of the church?

**December 31:** *Ps 96: 1-2, 11-13*
       *Jn 1: 1-18 (John's prologue)*

Matthew and Luke provide genealogies that
trace the human origins of Jesus back to David
and Adam, respectively. John, however, proposes that the Word, who became flesh in Jesus,
has existed with God from the beginning. This
magnificent truth enables us to have a share of
"Love following upon love."

• Read slowly through this passage, spending
  time with the verses that move you. Write your
  reflections in your journal.

• Make a list of concrete, achievable resolutions
  for the new year by noting your responses to
  the question: "What would I like to see different in my life next year at this time?" For
  each response, write down a plan for achieving
  your objectives.

• Pray for openness to change during the coming
  year.

**January 2:** *Ps 98: 1-4*
        *Jn 1: 19-28 (Jesus and John)*

We now return to a familiar theme: John the Baptist as precursor to the Messiah. Like John, it is important that we, too, recognize our limitations.

- How does selfishness limit your experiences of creation, work and relationships with other people?

- How do you usually respond to selfishness? Think about the next 24 hours and anticipate a time when selfishness will probably tempt you. Pray for the grace to respond in love.


**January 3:** *Ps 98: 1-6*
        *Jn 1: 29-34 (The lamb of God)*

Two important symbols describe the Messiah in today's reading. He is the lamb of God, whose sacrifice fulfills spiritually what the passover sacrificial lamb only anticipated. The dove is a symbol of the Holy Spirit, who rested upon the lamb, i.e., who animated Jesus.

- How do you feel about symbolic references to Jesus? Why do you think these symbols were important to John the Evangelist?

- In your imagination, picture yourself relaxing before a wellspring of flowing water. Pray that the Spirit may wash you clean of selfishness.

**January 4:** *Ps 98: 1, 7-9*
        *Jn 1: 35-42 (John introduces Jesus)*

John the Baptist perceived his role to be one of pointing the way to Christ. Our life is to reflect this same virtue through our work, play and relationships.

- Imagine yourself to be a disciple of John, listening to him as he points out the Messiah. See Jesus as he walks along the River Jordan; notice as he gazes at you in love; follow him as he takes you to the place where he lives. See where he lives and be with him there.

- Pray for the grace to become more discerning of the many places where God lives.


**January 5:** *Ps 100: 1-5*
        *Jn 1: 43-51 (Jesus, Philip and Nathanael)*

The calling of the apostles is one of the most revered of Christian traditions. In today's reading, we recount the traditions surrounding the call of Philip and Nathanael, who is probably identified in the other gospels as the apostle Bartholomew.

- How has God called you to be a follower of Jesus Christ? Who were his instruments? Recall the occasions that were turning points for you.

- How and why did you choose to become involved with the community of which you are now a member? Do you feel like inviting others to join?

**January 6:** *Ps 147: 12-15, 19-20*
       *Mk 1: 7-11 (Jesus is baptized by John)*

Even though many people believed that John the Baptist was the Messiah, John certainly knew his place. The gospel traditions concerning the Baptist and Jesus preserved a healthy respect for the unique mission and charismatic ministry of John, but point out that the ministry of Jesus in the Holy Spirit transcended it.

- Do you believe you have been baptized in the Holy Spirit? What does this term mean to you?

- Spend some time with the verse: "You are my beloved son/daughter. On you my favor rests." Pray for the grace to really feel God's favor.

**January 7:** *Ps 149: 1-6, 9*
       *Jn 2: 1-12 (The wedding at Cana)*

Jewish weddings are joyous occasions, and Jesus seems to have enjoyed these festivities as much, or more, than anyone else. The miracle of the transformed water symbolizes much more than his attempt to keep a party going, however; it points to the "new wine" which the Spirit produces in us and the wine poured out in the Eucharist, the gift of his flesh and blood.

- Is it hard for you to imagine Jesus having a good time? Is it hard for you to allow yourself to have fun?

- What does marriage mean to you? If you are married, let your spouse know today how important he or she is to you.

- Spend some time with the verse, "Do whatever he tells you," Mary's stance toward Jesus. Invite God to speak to you in your thoughts.

# Week After Epiphany

The word "epiphany" means manifestation, usually by the divine. In the liturgical calendar, the feast of the Epiphany commemorates the adoration of the infant Messiah by the three Magi. This feast calls to mind the universal dimensions of Christ's incarnation.

**Monday** (or January 7): *Ps 2: 7-8, 10-11*
*Mt 4: 12-17, 23-25 (Jesus heals)*

Matthew's gospel was addressed to a Jewish-Christian community, so it often quotes Old Testament prophets to show how Jesus fulfilled their predictions. In today's reading, we learn that a world in darkness has been visited by a healing Messiah.

- Does the phrase, "a land overshadowed by death," describe your perception of the world today? How does the light of Christ help illumine our world?

- Pray for the grace to be a source of healing to those around you today.

**Tuesday** (or January 8): *Ps 72: 1-4, 7-8*
*Mk 6: 34-44 (Jesus feeds thousands)*

Jesus was no mere spiritual Messiah. His concern for our spiritual well-being was matched by his understanding of the importance of our bodily needs. He knew well that hungry people are not overly interested in theology, so he fed them bread and fish.

• Spend some time with the passage, "You give them something to eat." How do you feel about being a co-redeemer with Christ?

• What kind of responsibility do you feel toward the poor and hungry in your community?

**Wednesday** (or January 9): *Ps 72: 1-2, 10, 12-13 Mk 6: 45-52 (Jesus on the water)*

Writing to gentiles, Mark emphasized miraculous events surrounding the ministry of Jesus since his audience had little appreciation for Jewish prophecy and its fulfillment in Christ. In today's passage, we read about one of the more unusual traditions preserved by the church: Jesus' walk on the water. Rather than being overawed by the accomplishment of this feat, we would do well to appreciate the more symbolic meanings conveyed by Mark.

• Why did Jesus spend time alone in prayer? Do you believe he had human needs just as we do?

• Spend some time with the verse, "Get hold of yourself. It is I. Do not be afraid." Let these words bring peace to your soul. Call them to mind through the day.

**Thursday** (or January 10): *Ps 72: 1-2, 14-15, 17*
  *Lk 4: 14-22 (Jesus at Nazareth)*

The Jewish synagogue was the place where people from the local community gathered to worship. As part of the service, people from the congregation were invited to read scripture passages. Often, the president of the synagogue invited distinguished guests to comment on them. It was often from that forum that Jesus addressed the Jews.

- Although Jesus obviously disagreed with the manner in which many aspects of Judaism were taught, he still went to the synagogue to worship with the people. What does this say to you about community and worship?

- Spend some time with the verse, "The Spirit of the Lord is upon me; therefore he has anointed me." Pray for the grace to believe these words.

**Friday** (or January 11): *Ps 147: 12-15, 19-20*
  *Lk 5: 12-16 (Jesus cures a leper)*

Leprosy is a disease well contained in our time, but during the time of Christ and until recently, it affected many. Because some forms are contagious, people who had leprosy were cast out of the community and were required to cry "Unclean!" when anyone approached. In isolation with other lepers, they were left to rot away. Only against this background can we appreciate the significance of Jesus' contact with lepers.

- How do you feel about your own contact with the "lower classes" of society? Do you avoid such contacts?

- Which lack of discipline is causing you to rot away spiritually? Ask Jesus to cure you.

**Saturday** (or January 12): *Ps 149: 1-6, 9*
　　　　*Jn 3: 22-30 (John points to Jesus)*

On this last day of the Advent-Christmas-Epiphany season, we again listen to the words of John the Baptist. "He must increase while I must decrease," John says, reflecting an attitude we should all take if the light of the Messiah is to become incarnate in our lives and transform this world.

- "The glory of God is humanity fully alive," St. Irenaeus wrote. Do you believe that this is an important statement about incarnation? Are you a fully alive person?

- Resolve to pay more attention to the vibrant people you come into contact with today. Ask one of them what the secret is behind their vitality.

# Ordinary
# Time

## After Christmas

We now begin the longest season of the church year: Ordinary Time. Depending on the date of Easter, five to seven weeks of this season precede Lent. During this time, we will be moving more or less systematically through the gospels of Mark, Matthew and Luke, respectively, focusing our attention on the "ordinary" ministry of Jesus between his baptism and crucifixion.

# First Week in Ordinary Time

**Monday:** *Ps 97: 1-2, 6-7, 9*
*Mk 1: 14-20 (Jesus begins his ministry)*

Mark's account of Jesus' early proclamation gives us a preview of all that is to follow. Jesus saw himself and his ministry as being essential to the coming of God's reign. He invites us to reform our lives if we, too, would be citizens of this kingdom.

• What's so good about the Good News? How is it different from other news?

• What kind of man must Jesus have been to attract four fishermen away from their tasks? Picture the call of these apostles in your imagination. Hear Jesus calling you, too, to follow him.

**Tuesday:** *Ps 8: 2, 5-9*
      *Mk 1: 21-28 (An exorcism)*

The people of Jesus' time believed that a myriad of kinds of evil spirits ruled the earth. Some of these spirits, it was believed, were angels that had fallen from grace, while others were evil people who had died. Jesus' healings were therefore understood in terms of displacing an evil spirit with the Holy Spirit.

- What kind of evil spirit keeps you from loving yourself as God loves you? What changes to yourself and/or the circumstances in which you live would make it easier for you to love yourself? Make a plan to begin working toward these changes.

- Spend some time with the verse, "What do you want of me, Jesus of Nazareth?" Listen to your thoughts as Jesus responds.

**Wednesday:** *Ps 105: 1-9*
      *Mk 1: 29-39 (A full day of ministering)*

The healing of Simon Peter's mother-in-law shows us that Jesus did not heal only to impress the masses. He extended his healing touch because people needed healing, and he traveled the countryside to touch many.

- Jesus' day was a mixture of solitude and action. Do you believe there is a good balance between these disciplines in your own life? How can you better balance them?

- Pray for the grace to be more willing to share yourself with others.

**Thursday:** *Ps 95: 6-11*
        *Mk 1: 40-45 (Jesus cures a leper)*

The gospels do not include a single account of Jesus refusing to heal someone who requested wholeness. The prayer of the leper in today's reading should be a model for all of us because the leper made his request in great humility and left the matter in Jesus' hands.

- Do you believe that God answers your prayers? What kinds of prayers do you find answered most often?

- What are some reasons why you are usually afraid to reach out to others? Pray for the grace to overcome these resistances.

**Friday:** *Ps 78: 3-4, 6-8*
        *Mk 2: 1-12 (Jesus can forgive sins)*

The scriptures teach us that sin is a power that keeps us from growing and which breaks up relationships. In today's reading, Jesus shows us that he can heal us from physical and spiritual paralyses.

- Some theologians have stated that we sin most often not by doing malicious and destructive things, but by settling for less than the best in ourselves. Think about it.

- What is paralyzing your love for family members? Pray for the grace to overcome any obstacles.

**Saturday:** *Ps 19: 8-10, 15*
      *Mk 2: 13-17 (An early confrontation)*

People loved Jesus and large crowds followed him. He was successful in attracting a group as diverse as fishermen, tax collectors, prostitutes, and even a member of the Sanhedrin. This success provoked jealousy among Jewish authorities, and led many of them to self-righteous judgments.

- Do you feel a need for God in your life? Why? (Why not?) What do you need God to do for you?

- What are the fruits of self-righteousness? Do any of these appear in your life?

# Second Week in Ordinary Time

**Monday:** *Ps 110: 1-4*
   *Mk 2: 18-22 (On new wine and new cloth)*

Jealousy prompted the disciples of John and the Pharisees to try to find fault with Jesus' spirituality. Rather than return the criticism, as he surely could have done, Jesus invited them to be open to a new way of doing God's will.

- Gibran says that Jesus stood before the world as the first man stood on the first day. Are you open to seeing the world in its daily newness?

- Resolve to stop many times today to appreciate creation and the people around you. Give thanks to God for these gifts. Begin now.

**Tuesday:** *Ps 111: 1-2, 4-5, 9-10*
   *Mk 2: 23-28 (Jesus, Lord of the sabbath)*

In Deuteronomy 23: 26, it is stated that Jews may pluck "some of your neighbor's grain with your hand, but do not put a sickle to it." This prevented the poor and starving from going hungry, but it was not to be done on the sabbath at any rate. Jesus shows us that human needs are more important than a rigid interpretation of the law.

- Do you go to church out of a sense of obligation? Evaluate your motives.

- How is Jesus the Lord of your Sunday experience?

**Wednesday:** *Ps 110: 1-4*
  *Mk 3: 1-6 (A healing and a confrontation)*

Today's reading describes a significant turning point in the ministry of Jesus. Jewish law forbade medical ministry on the sabbath except in critical life-saving situations. The man with the paralyzed hand was not in such critical condition, but Jesus healed him anyway. Because of this act of love, he earned the contempt of the legalistic Pharisees.

- Picture this confrontation in your imagination. Note the anger and indignation on Jesus' face as he addresses the authorities; see them responding to him from the heights of self-righteousness; experience the thrill of the moment when Jesus overrides the sabbath restrictions by saying, "Stretch out your hand." Note the gratitude on the man's face as his hand is healed.

- Are you self-assured yet humble in your efforts to love others?

**Thursday:** *Ps 40: 7-10, 17*
  *Mk 3: 7-12 (Jesus and the crowds)*

Again and again Mark tells of the crowds who followed Jesus for healing, teaching, and out of curiosity. Withdrawing from areas where conflict with the authorities might have brought a premature end to his ministry, Jesus took to the countryside, pursued by the crowds. He ministered on, undaunted.

- An ancient story tells of Satan instructing evil spirits in the art of damning souls. The most successful temptation was not to deny God's existence, or even the devil's existence, but "There's plenty of time." Why is this attitude so damning? Would you search for Jesus out in the "countryside"?

- Spend some time with the words of the psalmist: "Be still, and know that I am God."

**Friday:** *Ps 85: 10-14*
   *Mk 3: 13-19 (Jesus chooses the Twelve)*

Gospel parallels between Jesus and Moses are surely not coincidental. Moses went up on the mountain and brought back God's laws to the 12 tribes of Israel. Jesus went up on the mountain and returned with 12 men empowered to extend his healing love to a broken world.

- William Barclay notes that the apostles had no special gifts of intelligence or literacy, but they all loved Jesus and were willing to stand up for his cause. Are these qualities true of you?

- What kind of power does Jesus enable you to realize and extend?

- Thank God for the grace of being a disciple of Jesus Christ.

**Saturday:** *Ps 47: 2-3, 6-9*
   *Mk 3: 20-21 (Jesus and his family)*

The family of Jesus undoubtedly heard time and again of his extraordinary lifestyle, and they were no doubt concerned for his sanity. It must have been a painful moment for him and for them when they sought to take charge of him. God's call sometimes takes us to lonely places!

- Are you waiting for someone's approval to get on with your life?

- Thoreau wrote that most people "live lives of quiet desperation." Do you believe this is true?

- Pray for the grace to be willing to break out of the confines of oppressive conventionalities.

# Third Week in Ordinary Time

**Monday:** *Ps 98: 1-6*
*Mk 3: 22-30 (Sin against the Spirit)*

Today's gospel has Jesus confronting the scribes and their criticism of his exorcisms. Never one to back down from an opportunity to clarify God's truth, Jesus exposes the illogic of their arguments and issues that terrible warning about sinning against the Spirit, which means refusing to let the Spirit work in us.

- What would you like the Holy Spirit to help you to do/be? Ask God to help you to claim this grace.

- Jesus never backed down from a chance to teach. Are there times in your life when you could speak out more boldly for the sake of the kingdom?

**Tuesday:** *Ps 40: 2, 4, 7-8, 10-11*
*Mk 3: 31-35 (The true relatives of Jesus)*

Unlike the other evangelists, Mark does not apologize for Jesus' family and their misunderstanding of his mission. They had come to take him home, presumably to try to talk some sense into him. Jesus responded by claiming that he owed more allegiance to the family of God.

- How involved in family matters are you? Does your family identity complement or detract from your identity as a child of God?

• If you could change anything in your family, what would it be? For what are you most thankful?

**Wednesday:** *Ps 110: 1-4*
     *Mk 4: 1-20 (Parable of the Sower)*

Jesus tried to teach about spiritual matters by using analogies from human experience. His parables were attempts to tease the mind into understanding his message.

• Apply this parable to your present situation, letting the seed be the word of God and the field be your own heart (rather than society).

• What are examples of footpaths, rocky ground, thorns and fertile ground in your own life? How can you better cultivate your field to give the word fertile ground?

**Thursday:** *Ps 24: 1-6*
     *Mk 4: 21-25 (Nothing is hidden from God)*

Truth and love cannot be forever suppressed, Jesus tells us. Like light shining in darkness, the works of a disciple of Jesus will not remain hidden. It is precisely these works which will prevent the darkness of sin from completely overtaking the world.

• Emerson wrote, "Be careful of what you want, for you will get it." What are you really seeking in your everyday involvements? Why?

- Pray for the grace of purity of intention.

**Friday:** *Ps 37: 3-6, 23-24, 39-40*
       *Mk 4: 26-34 (The mustard seed)*

The kingdom of God will conquer, Jesus assures us, for God's will is sovereign. Grace reaches deeper than sin; evil will be uprooted.

- Do you believe that you have made progress in your life in Christ during the past few months? Years? How has grace transformed you?

- Do you feel hopeful about God's kingdom conquering? Why? (Why not?) How does this affect your everyday attitude?

**Saturday:** *Lk 1: 69-75*
        *Mk 4: 35-41 (Calming a storm)*

This is a very human scene: Jesus sleeping, the disciples afraid of a storm at sea. Mark tells us that peace came to the disciples when they realized that Jesus was with them.

- Over what storms in your life would you like the peace of God to reign?

- Spend some time letting the saying, "Quiet! Be Still!" deepen your peace.

# Fourth Week in Ordinary Time

**Monday:** *Ps 31: 20-24*
   *Mk 5: 1-20 (Exorcising a hopeless case)*

Jesus had ventured into an area inhabited by non-Jews. This story of the demoniac and the swineherd reminds us that Jesus has come to save all people, even the lowest of classes and the most hopeless of cases. The price of a human soul is worth more to God than anything else in the world.

• Let your imagination recreate this scene for you. How did Jesus look at the demoniac? Hear him saying to you, "Unclean spirits, begone!"

• What kind of involvement do you have with the poor, the underprivileged, and the outcasts of society?

**Tuesday:** *Ps 22: 26-32*
   *Mk 5: 21-43 (More healings and resuscitations)*

Jesus never refused anyone's request for healing. His miraculous deeds demonstrated the presence of the kingdom of God in the midst of humanity. Today's reading reveals God's desire to make people whole.

• The woman touched Jesus in such a manner that she drew power from him.

- Why did Jesus want to know who touched him?

- Has anyone ever touched you or someone you know with expectant faith? How did you (they) respond?

**Wednesday:** *Ps 103: 1-2, 13-14, 17-18*
     *Mk 6: 1-6 (Jesus rejected by his own)*

The response of the people of Nazareth to Jesus holds an important lesson for us. They thought they knew him, and they tried to make him conform to their own ideas. Consequently, they did not recognize him for who he was, and he could not touch them. We, too, need to be cautious about thinking we know and understand Jesus completely.

- Louis Evely once wrote, "As soon as we think we know someone, we have ceased to love them." How does this relate to the people of Nazareth? How does it relate to your relationship with Jesus? With your family and friends?

- Pray for the grace to discover newness in God, yourself and others.

**Thursday:** *Ps 48: 2-4, 9-11*
     *Mk 6: 7-13 (The Twelve sent out)*

It is important to note that Jesus sent the apostles out in pairs. From the first, the importance of support in ministry was emphasized. So was traveling light, free from unnecessary burdens. Simplicity of lifestyle and fellowship in community remain important values for Christians.

- Do you have a simple lifestyle? What adjustments do you feel are in order so that you might experience the freedom that the simple life offers?

- Do you have the support you need to minister in your daily life? Pray for the grace to experience support from friends.

**Friday:** *Ps 27: 1, 3, 5, 8-9*
     *Mk 6: 14-29 (Herod and John)*

Herod had tried to silence the voice of his own conscience by imprisoning and killing John the Baptist. This passage points out the utter superficiality of Herod's life, while issuing a subtle warning about the impossibility of suppressing God's intentions.

- Herod was trapped in a role, unable to find holiness because of his life situation. How are you like him? How are you different?

- Pray for the grace to break out of roles that confine you.

**Saturday:** *Ps 23: 1-6*
        *Mk 6: 30-34 (The people ruin a retreat)*

Jesus saw that his tired band of disciples needed to get away and be with him. He set out to take them on a private retreat, as it were, but found his plans frustrated. Note the manner in which he readjusts his concern.

- How do you usually respond to interruptions and frustrated plans? Do you see them as occasions to minister?

- Review your plans for today and anticipate times when they might go awry. How will you respond?

- Pray for the grace to recognize opportunities to love and grow.

# Fifth Week in Ordinary Time

**Monday:** *Ps 104: 1-6, 10, 12, 24, 35*
  *Mk 6: 53-56 (The people seek Jesus out)*

Without the aid of television, radio, or newspaper advertisements, Jesus' reputation spread. People found in him one who could meet their needs, so they sought him out.

- How convinced are you of your need of God? What do you need most from God?

- Spend time thanking God for graces you usually take for granted.

**Tuesday:** *Ps 8: 4-9*
  *Mk 7: 1-13 (The injustice of certain traditions)*

Although the Pharisees are constantly criticized in the gospels, they were popular religious leaders, similar in stature among their communities to today's parish priests. Their major fault lay in their legalistic observance of the Law even to the point of hurting people or ignoring human needs in the process. Jesus points out a few examples of this in today's reading.

- Can you think of an example of legalism in your own experience in the church? How does this affect your involvement in the church now?

- What criteria did Jesus employ for evaluating the justice of a law?

**Wednesday:** *Ps 104: 1-2, 27-30*
          *Mk 7: 14-23 (On what makes for*
          *uncleanness)*

Jewish dietary laws were initially established for a variety of reasons, many related more to health than to piety. It was because many Jews believed that holiness was a matter of observing such rules and regulations, rather than purity of heart, that Jesus criticized the dietary law observances.

• Let your imagination take you to the recesses of your heart. What do you see there?

• Pray for the grace to recognize your mixed motives.

**Thursday:** *Ps 128: 1-5*
          *Mk 7: 24-30 (Daughter of a gentile woman*
          *healed)*

Jesus' seemingly harsh rebuke to the woman is softened somewhat when we realize that the word he used for dog actually means house pet. His confrontation with the woman drew out a faith response from her and taught his disciples that God's grace is for all people, not just Jews.

• What kind of "demon" is straining relationships in your family? What does love require to exorcise this demon?

• Pray for the grace to be more loving to family members.

**Friday:** *Ps 32: 1-2, 5-7*
    *Mk 7: 31-37 (Healing a deaf man)*

Again we see Jesus encouraging people to silence regarding a miracle. To Jesus, miracles were signs of the presence of God in our midst, and he did not want this to be misinterpreted on account of sensationalism.

• Is there anyone you know who needs to hear words of love from you but has not because of your hesitation to reach out?

• Hear Jesus saying, "Ephphatha! Be opened!" What do you need to be more open to?

**Saturday:** *Ps 90: 2-6, 12-13*
    *Mk 8: 1-10 (Second miracle of the loaves)*

The multiplication of the loaves and fish is often considered a foreshadowing of the eucharistic Bread of Life. Just as Jesus gave sustenance to people through his teaching, healing and miraculous feedings, so now does he continue to nourish us in a very special way through his presence in the Eucharist.

• Make a list of the excuses you usually make to distance yourself from responding to the needs of the poor and hungry.

• Thank God for the grace of a substantial diet.

# Sixth Week in Ordinary Time

**Monday:** *Ps 50: 1, 8, 16-17, 20-21*
*Mk 8: 11-13 (Pharisees seek a sign)*

The Pharisees expected the Messiah to manifest certain glorious signs, and their request for such a sign from Jesus was an attempt to test him. Jesus rejects their request, hurt at their distrust and disturbed that their faith was so shallow.

- If you could ask God to manifest some sign to deepen your faith, what would you ask for? How would this help you? What would it say about God?

- Pray for faith in a God of love.

**Tuesday:** *Ps 29: 1-4, 9-10*
*Mk 8: 14-21 (Jesus warns his disciples to be on guard)*

Although Jesus' disciples loved him dearly, there were times when they found it hard to comprehend the symbolic language of their Master. When Jesus tried to warn them about the influence of the Pharisees and Herod, they misinterpreted his words. They really did not understand him.

- List a few destructive "yeasts" in our society that erode faith. Which of these do you struggle with most intensely?

- Thank God for things you have taken for granted lately.

**Wednesday:** *Ps 116: 12-15, 18-19*
         *Mk 8: 22-26 (Jesus heals a blind man)*

In this passage we see Jesus giving individual consideration to a man brought to him by the crowd. Similarly, we must remember that our God, who is present to all of creation, nonetheless gives each one of us full attention.

- Leo Buscaglia said: "If you don't touch, you're out of touch." How do you feel about touching those you love? How do you feel about being touched?

- Recreate this gospel scene in your imagination. Hear Jesus saying, "Can you see anything?" Ask him to heal your blindnesses.

**Thursday:** *Ps 102: 16-23, 29*
         *Mk 8: 27-33 (Who do you say he is?)*

This passage marks a turning point in Mark's gospel: The community, through Peter, asserts its faith in Jesus as the Messiah and, in turn, challenges all people to answer this most important of all questions for themselves.

- Who do you say Jesus was/is? Why do you believe this?

- You might find it helpful to write a short letter to Jesus. Thank him for being who he is for you.

**Friday:** *Ps 33: 10-15*
*Mk 8: 34-9: 1 (The way of the cross)*

Following the way of loving service will not always be easy, Jesus promises. But those who persevere in love, even through times of suffering, will become a new creation.

- What does the cross mean to you? How do you experience it in your life?

- What does it mean to "lose your life" for the sake of the gospel.

**Saturday:** *Ps 145: 2-5, 10-11*
*Mk 9: 2-13 (Christ's glory revealed)*

In a moment of profound intimacy, the core leadership of the apostles — Peter, James and John — is given a glimpse into the depths of Jesus' heart. They recognize in him the fulfillment of the Law and the Prophets and hear the call to obey him as their Lord. Jesus, who had recently promised them the cross, now gives them a promise of the glory to come.

- Have you ever felt as Peter, James and John must have felt on the mountain of transfiguration? Try to recall the circumstances and invite those feelings to renew you.

- Spend time with the passage, "This is my Son. . . . Listen to him." After a few moments, write down what you think Jesus is telling you.

# The
# Season of
# Lent

During Lent we continue to reflect upon the mysteries celebrated during Advent and Christmas. The incarnation of God in the person of Jesus Christ is made fully manifest through Jesus' suffering, death and resurrection. In order to prepare us properly to reverence Jesus as Lord and Savior, the church encourages prayer, fasting and mortification of self-indulgent passions. In recent years the importance of positive acts of love and mercy has also been emphasized.

**Ash Wednesday:** *Ps 51: 3-6, 12-14, 17*
        *Mk 6: 1-6, 16-18 (Be sincere!)*

Gaining the esteem of others is something we all desire. But Jesus makes it clear that our religious acts should be done to bring us closer to God, not to impress people. Some of the examples of hypocrisy he gives refer to practices of the Pharisees.

* How important is it to you that others know you are committed to following Jesus Christ? What are your motives for letting others know that you are a Christian?

* In what ways does your heavenly Father repay you for your prayer in private? Spend some time thanking God for these graces.

**Thursday After Ash Wednesday:** *Ps 1: 1-4, 6*
         *Lk 9: 22-25 (Take up your cross!)*

Jesus tried to help his disciples realize that his commitment to love would lead him into a fatal conflict with the authorities of his day. Dying to ourselves for the sake of love will lead us, with Jesus, to new life.

• Make a list of some of the attributes of the old self which you need to change for the sake of love. Which of these attributes most frustrates your efforts at loving?

• Pray for the grace to change destructive behaviors.


**Friday After Ash Wednesday:** *Ps 54: 3-6, 18-19*
        *Mt 9: 14-15 (Jesus the bridegroom)*

Jesus viewed his coming as a time of grace, and he believed that this ought to be celebrated. Many times he likened God's kingdom to a wedding feast, where people rejoiced and had fun. The day would come, however, when fasting would be appropriate. That time is now.

• Read Isaiah 58: 1-9 (today's first reading) for a better understanding of the kind of fast that God desires. How can you better exemplify this spirit of fasting in your lifestyle?

• Pray for the grace to hunger for the things of God.

**Saturday After Ash Wednesday:** *Ps 86: 1-6*
        *Lk 5: 27-32 (The call of Levi)*

Tax collectors were men commissioned by the Romans to exact from the peoples they governed monies and property owed Rome. Then, as now, tax collectors were despised by the people. Levi, a Jew, was considered a traitor by other Jews, but Jesus nonetheless chose him to be a disciple, a member of his inner circle. Jesus' call elicited gratitude from Levi and scandalized the Pharisees and scribes.

- What does Jesus mean when he talks of healthy and sick people? In what group do you consider yourself? How are you sick?

- Spend some time re-creating this scene in your imagination. Sense the rejection Levi feels from his fellow Jews; note a change when he sees Jesus paying attention to him; hear Jesus saying to him, and to you, "Follow me."

# First Week in Lent

**Monday:** *Ps 19: 8-10, 15*
*Mt 25: 31-46 (Who are the saved?)*

It has often been said that the clearest indication of our relationship with God is deduced from our relationships with human beings. In today's reading, Jesus makes it clear that we will be judged on the basis of how we have treated others — even the outcasts of society.

- If you were to die today, do you believe you would be included in the company of the sheep, or the goats?

- Is there any person or any racial or religious group against whom you harbor resentments and harsh judgments?

- Pray for the grace to see all people as children of God.

**Tuesday:** *Ps 34: 4-7, 16-19*
*Mt 6: 7-15 (The Lord's Prayer)*

This most famous of all prayers is rather a formula for prayer. Its movements include acknowledgment of God as creator, praise, hope for the kingdom, affirmation of the importance of life on earth, petition for our needs, requests for forgiveness, and protection from evil. This passage is concluded with a sobering reminder that our experience of God's forgiveness is contingent on our own willingness to forgive.

• Spend a few moments with each line of the Lord's Prayer, adding your own prayers to each verse. When you ask for your daily bread and for forgiveness, be specific in your requests.

**Wednesday:** *Ps 51: 3-4, 12-13, 18-19*
        *Lk 11: 29-32 (The sign of Jonah)*

Jesus' condemnation of the attitude of the crowds was intended to move them to faith. He saw that they did not really hunger for the things of God, but wanted demonstrations of supernatural power instead. The Queen of Sheba and the Ninevites were pagans who recognized the workings of God in holy Jews and reformed their lives accordingly. Jesus holds them out as models to us.

• What are some signs of God's presence that are most meaningful to you? What are signs you need to try harder to recognize?

• Pray for the grace to recognize God's workings in yourself and others.

**Thursday:** *Ps 138: 1-3, 7-8*
        *Mt 7: 7-12 (Ask, seek, knock)*

Jesus reveals to us a God who is generous and responsive. This does not exempt us from searching for ways to grow closer to him, however. It is in the searching and asking that we discover ourselves and God's goodness.

- What are you seeking from God? From your family members?

- How would you like others to treat you? Make a list, then commit yourself to treating others likewise.

**Friday:** *Ps 130: 1-8*
*Mt 5: 20-26 (On forgiveness and reconciliation)*

Today's reading introduces an important lesson. We learn that anger can separate us from others and therefore we ought to control it by striving to be reconciled with those who are the objects of our anger.

- What (or who) most often causes you anger? How do you usually handle your anger? Are your expectations about others always reasonable? How can you change them?

- Make a commitment to reconcile with someone you're angry with (or who is angry with you).

**Saturday:** *Ps 119: 1-5, 7-8*
*Mt 5: 43-48 (Love your enemies)*

Jesus teaches that the only way to break the seemingly never-ending cycle of hatred and revenge is to begin to treat enemies as fellow children of God. The commandment to love our enemies is one of the most unique of all Jesus' teachings and, unfortunately, the most neglected.

- Voltaire wrote that patriotism really means hating every other country but your own. Do you sense this kind of spirit in the world around you? How does it affect you?

- Spend some time in prayer for people with whom you do not get along particularly well. Ask for the grace to begin to love them.

# Second Week in Lent

**Monday:** *Ps 79: 8-9, 11, 13*
      *Lk 6: 36-38 (Do not judge)*

Today's reading is one of the most sobering in scripture. Jesus proposes that we evaluate our lives using the same criteria we use to evaluate others. How do we fare?

- Old sayings have it that "What goes around comes around," and, "You will get out of life no more nor less than you put into it." Are these true in your experience?

- Why are Christians called to be compassionate?

- Pray for the grace to see others as God sees them.


**Tuesday:** *Ps 50: 8-9, 16-17, 21, 23*
      *Mt 23: 1-12 (On servant leadership)*

The principle of servant leadership has it that one's ability to use authority responsibly is in direct relationship with one's service to others. Authority assumed for reasons other than service will result in all kinds of abuses and superficialities.

- Which title best fits Jesus: king, ruler, servant, master, prophet, teacher, philosopher, rabbi? Why did you pick the answer you did?

• Do you think of yourself as a servant? Whom do you serve?

**Wednesday:** *Ps 31: 5-6, 14-16*
   *Mt 20: 17-28 (A mother's request)*

It is obvious to us today that the mother of Zebedee's sons did not understand what Jesus' kingdom was about. Her request was made in good faith — not an unusual one from a Jewish mother trying to see to it that her sons get the best treatment possible. The indignation which followed was turned into a teachable moment by Jesus.

• What are some of your professional ambitions? How important is it to you that you realize them? Why?

• Pray for the grace to accept failures as gracefully as successes.

**Thursday:** *Ps 1: 1-4, 6*
   *Lk 16: 19-31 (The rich man and Lazarus)*

The parable of the rich man and Lazarus teaches us that the real value of our lives must be seen against a backdrop of the inevitability of death and the prospect of judgment by God. The surest way to guarantee repose in the "bosom of Abraham" is to love God and neighbor.

• What kinds of situations make you feel insecure? When do you feel most secure? What is your primary source of security?

- How do you feel about the prospect of evaluating your life before God after death?

**Friday:** *Ps 105: 16-21*
   *Mt 21: 33-46 (Parable of the wicked tenants)*

Jesus did not hide behind polite facades when love required that truth be spoken. In today's parable, he reveals his knowledge of the intentions of Jewish authorities to dispose of him, yet continues to invite them to recognize God working through him.

- God has entrusted us with the cultivation of a vineyard, his kingdom. Who are the faithful tenants today? Who are the unfaithful ones? How can you tell one from the other?

- If the Master of the vineyard were to come today, what do you think he would say to you? Spend some time listening.

**Saturday:** *Ps 103: 1-4, 9-12*
   *Lk 15: 1-3, 11-32 (The Prodigal Son)*

Today's parable is extremely rich in meaning. The marked contrasts between the attitudes of the father, the faithful son, and the prodigal son tell us much about God and ourselves.

- List some of the areas in your life where you are faithful to God. Give also a few of the reasons *why* you are faithful in each of those areas.

- Write a short characterization of the father in the parable.

- Pray for the grace to know that you are a forgiven sinner.

# Third Week in Lent

**Monday:** *Ps 42: 2, 3; 43: 3-4*
*Lk 4: 24-30 (A confrontation in Nazareth)*

Since Jesus grew up in Nazareth, it is understandable that the people of this town thought they knew him better than most. They could not accept his special ministry, however, so Jesus confronted them for their lack of faith.

- Have you ever felt boxed-in or limited by close friends and family members who are interested only in that part of you with which they are comfortable? What is your response to this?

- Is there some friend or family member whom you need to get to know better? Make a commitment to communicate with that person about something new this week.

**Tuesday:** *Ps 25: 4-9*
*Mt 18: 21-35 (The depths of forgiveness)*

Today's reading continues developing a theme that runs through the entire Lenten season: forgiveness and reconciliation. Jesus' admonition to forgive 77 or 70 times seven times is not to be taken literally, of course; Jesus is simply using exaggeration to make an important point.

- Is there anyone in your life you need to forgive? Ask for guidance to think of a creative way to let that person know that you forgive him or her.

- Is there anyone in your life whom you feel owes you forgiveness? Is a reconciliation with this person possible?

**Wednesday:** *Ps 147: 12-16, 19-20*
*Mt 5: 17-19 (God's commandments are eternal)*

Jesus taught us that God's commandments were not given to us to analyze or to evaluate their worth in terms of our own desires. Rather, God's commandments were given to help form our desires; they are to be obeyed.

- With which of God's commandments do you struggle most often? How will this struggle probably take place today?

- Pray for the grace to become more obedient to God's commandments.

**Thursday:** *Ps 95: 1-2, 6-9*
*Lk 11: 14-23 (The reign of God is upon you)*

The gospels reveal that it was impossible for people to encounter Jesus and remain indifferent toward him. This passage shows that some people interpreted his influence and power as arising from demonic sources. Jesus exposed the irrationality of their accusation and invited them to join him in gathering the kingdom harvest.

- What do you believe it means to be "with" Jesus? Whom do you believe is with him?

- What kind of conscience guards the doors of your soul? List some of the values that are most important to you.

**Friday:** *Ps 81: 6-11, 14, 17*
     *Mk 12: 28-34 (The greatest commandment)*

True religion is much simpler than we usually make it. In this passage Jesus teaches us that God is not a philosophical proposition to be figured out, but a Being to be loved. Likewise, other human beings are to be loved even as we love ourselves.

- Make a list of the people and things you love most in this world according to their importance to you. Where does God come in? How can you draw closer to God?

- Do you love yourself? How does your self-love affect your relationships?

**Saturday:** *Ps 51: 3-4, 18-21*
     *Lk 18: 9-14 (The Pharisee and the Publican)*

In this parable of contrasts, we get an idea of what our attitude toward God should be. Because everything we have and are and ever will be is made possible because of grace, we should approach God in humble thanksgiving.

- Hear the Pharisee saying, "I give you thanks, O God, that I am not like the rest of men." Does this attitude resonate in you? Which people or groups of people do you believe you are superior to?

- Spend some time with the publican's prayer, "O God, be merciful to me, a sinner." Repeat this prayer again and again as you breathe slowly and let the words draw you to God's mercy.

# Fourth Week in Lent

**Monday:** *Ps 30: 2-6, 11-13*
   *Jn 4: 43-54 (The official's son is healed)*

The royal official in this reading was a gentile — a non-Jew, but his faith in Jesus to heal his sick boy transcended all racial and credal boundaries. This is the kind of simple faith to which we are called.

- Picture in your imagination the scene between Jesus and the official. Hear the man continue pleading, despite Jesus' objections. See Jesus' face as he recognizes the great faith the official has in him.

- Rise from your prayer position and begin walking slowly around the room. With each step you take, believe that God will grant you the strength to persevere in love through any problems you might be having now. After awhile, relax again and give thanks to God for the gift of faith.

**Tuesday:** *Ps 46: 2-6, 8-9*
   *Jn 5: 1-3, 5-16 (A healing in Jerusalem)*

Jesus found people in great suffering and abandonment everywhere. In today's reading he notes the faith and hope in a man who had been suffering for 38 years. Jesus heals him, but is criticized for doing so because it was the sabbath, a day when such works were forbidden.

- What "moving waters" are you waiting for so that you can get about the business of living fully? How is this affecting you now?

- Hear Jesus saying to you, "Get up, take up your sleeping mat, and walk."

## Wednesday: *Ps 145: 8-9, 13-14, 17-18*
   *Jn 5: 17-30 (Jesus' credentials)*

When the Jews criticized Jesus for healing on the sabbath, he replied that his Father, who goes on working always, is not bound by sabbath restrictions. He went on to invite the Jews to recognize the power at work in him as being critical for life and death.

- Read this passage over slowly, spending time with whatever verse catches your attention. Do not try to reflect on every phrase.

- Spend some time with the words, "My aim is to do not my own will, but the will of him who sent me." Repeat them again and again as you allow your will to merge with God's.

## Thursday: *Ps 106: 19-23*
   *Jn 5: 31-47 (More on Jesus' credentials)*

When Jesus claimed to be doing God's work, it was only natural that the Jews should ask him for proof that this was in fact the case. Crackpots and false messiahs abounded then, as now. Jesus pointed to the testimony of Moses and of John the

Baptist, the scriptures, and the works that he did as evidence that his claims were not unfounded.

• What kind of reasoning supports your own faith in Jesus? How can you deepen your understanding of who Jesus is?

• What does human approval mean to you? How important is it in your involvements in the church?

• Pray for the grace to be more detached from the need for human approval.

**Friday:** *Ps 34: 17-21, 23*
         *Jn 7: 1-2, 10, 25-30 (On Christ's origins)*

The Jews had many preconceptions as to where the Messiah would come from, what he would be like, and what he would do. Many of these preconceptions prevented them from recognizing Jesus as the one they had prayed for.

• Have you (like Jesus) ever been misjudged and limited by others who drew hasty conclusions about you? Is this happening on a regular basis even now? How are you handling it?

• What do you do to prevent your first impressions about other people from limiting your relationship with them?

• Pray for the grace to let God be God in your life.

**Saturday:** *Ps 7: 2-3, 9-12*
*Jn 7: 40-53 (The people's response to Jesus)*

It was obvious to many people that Jesus was an extraordinary man. Still they tried to cast him in every other role except the one which he himself proposed: that of God's Son.

- What do you think the temple guards experienced as they listened to Jesus? Have you ever experienced this? Get in touch with those memories and feelings.

- Make a commitment to do something special in the next week to help you draw closer to God.

# Fifth Week in Lent

**Monday:** *Ps 23: 1-6*
*Jn 8: 1-11 (Jesus and the adulterous woman)*

Today's reading reveals depths of human malice that sickened Jesus. Having caught a woman (where was the man?) in the act of adultery, the authorities brought her to Jesus, attempting to pit his mercy against his justice and catch him in a trap. A pious tradition has it that Jesus wrote on the ground to spell out to each of the accusers what their specific sins were, causing them to leave shamefaced.

• In your imagination, place yourself as a bystander observing this scene between the authorities, Jesus and the woman. Note the self-righteousness on the face of the authorities; watch Jesus writing on the ground and glancing up at each official in turn; feel the gratitude in the woman's eyes; hear Jesus speaking words of forgiveness to her.

• Write down your impressions from the imagination exercise. Note especially your impressions of Jesus.

**Tuesday:** *Ps 102: 2-3, 16-21*
*Jn 8: 21-30 (Jesus is one with the Father)*

Unlike Matthew, Mark and Luke, John often has Jesus involved in long, profound dialogues with unbelievers and authorities. This is a method he uses to articulate his community's understanding of who Jesus is in the face of persecution from Jews and Romans alike. In today's reading, Jesus speaks of the revelation that is to come when he is lifted up, or crucified.

- Spend some time with the passage, "He who sent me is with me, and has not left me to myself." Become aware of God's nearness and love for you.

- Make a resolution to let a special person in your life know that you care about him or her.

**Wednesday:** *Dn 3: 52-56*
        *Jn 8: 31-42 (The meaning of freedom)*

It is a paradox that untamed passions bring enslavement, whereas self-discipline brings freedom. Jesus promises that the discipline of living according to his teaching will bring freedom, for he is the Son who reveals to us the human way to God.

- What does freedom mean to you? What kinds of situations restrict your experience of freedom? What are some of the limits of your exercise of freedom?

- Make a resolution to discipline a passion that has caused you to feel unfree. Pray for the grace to have control over this passion.

**Thursday:** *Ps 105: 4-9*
       *Jn 8: 51-59 (The eternal origin of the Christ)*

The meeting of the human and divine in Jesus shall be forever a mystery, an inexhaustible truth. Certainly the human Jesus was born of Mary in space and time. John, however, reminds us today that the great I AM (Yahweh), whose knowledge is of eternity, also lives in Jesus. The Jews considered such a belief blasphemous and attempted to stone Jesus.

• What does today's reading have to say to those who consider Jesus only a great man, or else one of several incarnations of God along with Buddha and Mohammed, for example?

• Spend some time with the passage, "If I glorify myself, that glory comes to nothing. He who gives me glory is the Father." Write your impressions.

**Friday:**  *Ps 18: 2-7*
           *Jn 10: 31-42 (Jesus confronts his critics)*

Before the Jews rush to hasty conclusions, Jesus again reminds them that his works back his words and he invites them to reconsider their unfounded judgments against him. When they reply by trying to arrest him, he escapes, for he is not yet ready to make his decisive confrontation.

• To whom do the works you do day in and day out testify? To whom do you give the glory?

• Spend some time with the passage, "The Father is in me and I in him"  and its equivalent in 1 Jn 4: 4, "He who is in you is greater than any power in the world." Pray for the grace to be filled with this power.

**Saturday:** *Jer 31: 10-13*
*Jn 11: 45-57 (Jesus is condemned to die)*

This passage comes after the raising of Lazarus from the dead, an event which caused many Jews to put their faith in Jesus. The Sanhedrin was the great religious council, a gathering of prominent religious leaders similar to our own bishops' council meetings today. Caiaphas, the designated leader, proposed that killing Jesus was preferable to the destruction of the status quo. John turns this statement into a cryptic prophecy of Jesus' redemptive death and resurrection.

• Leo Tolstoy wrote, "If, by doing God's will, I help to bring about the dissolution of the existing order of things, then the existing order of things needs to be changed." How does this statement differ from that of Caiaphas? Is there a middle ground between the two upon which a Christian might stand in good faith?

• Do you believe that any of the civil laws of your government conflict with the values of Christ? What stand do you take in such a conflict?

# Holy Week

**Monday:** *Ps 27: 1-3, 13-14*
  *Jn 12: 1-11 (Mary anoints Jesus)*

We begin this Holy Week with a reading that anticipates Jesus' death and burial. Earlier in John's gospel, Mary had shown her choice for sitting at the feet of Jesus while Martha, her sister, criticized her for not helping with housework. In today's passage, Judas criticizes Mary for her extravagant expression of love for Jesus, but Jesus rebukes him and affirms her display as prophetic of his burial.

- Do you believe that money and time spent on Christian art and on church worship space is scandalous in a world where so many are poor?

- Make a resolution to demonstrate your love for another person in an extravagant way for the glory of God.

**Tuesday:** *Ps 71: 1-6, 15, 17*
  *Jn 13: 21-33, 36-38 (Judas betrays Jesus)*

It is very likely that Judas was a man with many admirable qualities, else Jesus would not have chosen him to be an apostle. Judas did not like the way things were turning out, however, and probably hoped that the confrontation he was forcing between Jesus and the authorities would put some "sense" into Jesus. Judas' plan backfired, as we know, but Jesus saw his betrayal as the beginning of his hour of glory.

- What are some of the ways in which you betray Jesus? Make a list and pray for forgiveness.

99

- Spend some time with the passage, "(Where I am) you cannot follow me now; later on you shall come after me."

**Wednesday:** *Ps 69: 8-10, 21-22, 31, 33-34*
*Mt 26: 14-25 (The Passover meal begins)*

The Passover was a Jewish feast recalling the historical exodus of the Jews and their liberation from the land of Egypt. Jesus, a Jew, deeply loved this tradition and chose to share it with his most intimate friends, the apostles. This particular Passover meal will take on a new meaning in the light of the crucifixion and resurrection of Jesus.

- How important to you is the sharing of a meal with friends and/or family? How does the sharing of a meal help to build relationships?

- Look into the possibility of sharing a Passover meal with a church group or community.

**Holy Thursday** *(evening Mass): Ps 116*
*Jn 13: 1-15 (Jesus washes the apostles' feet)*

This is Jesus' final evening with his apostles, and it is time to begin sharing farewells and preparing for the treachery to come. Matthew, Mark and Luke emphasized the sharing of the bread and wine, with Jesus asking the apostles to remember him in that manner. John chose to recall Jesus washing the apostles' feet as the last symbolic intimacy he shared with them.

- Bishop Sheen once wrote that although we have Jesus' example of the washing of the apostles' feet as a model of service, it is difficult to find people today fighting for the towel. Is this true of you? What are some of the "lowly" jobs at home and at work you avoid because you feel they are "beneath your dignity"?

- Pray for the grace to be "washed" clean of false pride.

**Good Friday:** *Ps 31*
   *Jn 18: 1-19: 42 (Jesus arrested, condemned, crucified)*

Crucifixion was not the kind of death a community would choose for its hero. Roman crucifixion was reserved for the most heinous criminals in society and was intended to discourage other criminals from testing the Pax Romana. Since the Jews were not permitted to carry out the death sentence, they needed to convince the Roman procurator, Pontius Pilate, that Jesus deserved to die. Pilate seems to have been reluctant to comply, but he finally gave in and Jesus was "lifted up."

- After reading through John's passion narrative, spend some time reflecting on the cost of loving as Jesus loved.

- Bonhoeffer, a Protestant pastor who was killed by the Nazis, wrote that when Jesus Christ calls a person, he bids him or her to come and die. How do you feel about this?

- Pray for the grace to be willing to lay down your life today for the sake of love.

# The
## Season
### of
# Easter

Easter is the day of Christ's victory over sin and death. Baptism initiates us into fellowship with Jesus and gives us the right to stand before God and plead for the graces won by him. During the season of Easter, we will consider the implications of being an Easter people—a people who live in full confidence that power will be given us to live a life free from the shackles of shame, fear and despair.

# First Week of Easter

**Monday:** *Ps 16: 1-2, 5, 7-11*
*Mt 28: 8-15 (Jesus appears to the women)*

In Matthew's resurrection narratives, Jesus appears first to women and commissions them to go to the apostles. They are the first evangelists bringing the Good News of the resurrection to the world—an awesome elevation of the role of women in a male-dominated culture. The story of the theft of the body by Jesus' disciples reminds us that belief in the resurrection was disputed by some even from the beginning.

- Do you believe Jesus of Nazareth was raised from the dead? Do you believe that you, too, will be—and are even now being—raised to new life? What does that mean to you?

- How can you communicate the joy of Easter to those with whom you will be interacting today?

105

**Tuesday:** *Ps 33: 4-5, 18-20, 22*
> *Jn 20: 11-18 (Jesus appears to Mary of Magdala)*

Mary of Magdala was judged harshly by society, yet she was one of the few who followed Jesus to the cross. In today's reading, Jesus appears to her and commissions her to tell his disciples that he is risen. Those who love deeply are those who will see Christ, as Mary discovered.

- In your imagination, be with Mary through this passage. Feel the depths of her grief as she approaches the tomb, then discovers that Jesus' corpse is gone. Experience her longing for Jesus as she pleads with him (the gardener) to tell her where she can find the corpse and get it back. Note her joy when Jesus calls her name. Adore Jesus with her as she embraces him.

- Pray for the grace to believe that Jesus is truly risen.

**Wednesday:** *Ps 105: 1-4, 6-9*
> *Lk 24: 13-35 (The road to Emmaus)*

Those who loved Jesus were crushed by his scandalous death. Whatever he had promised them concerning his resurrection must have been poorly understood, for his followers were deeply shaken when they learned that his tomb was empty. The disciples' experience on the road to

Emmaus gives us an idea as to how their sorrow was turned to joy.

- Imagine yourself walking down a lonely road with Jesus at your side. Pour out your heart to him; tell him what sorts of things have been weighing heavily upon you. Write in your journal the response you believe he is giving you.

- What is the significance of the verses concerning the breaking of the bread? How important to you is breaking bread with other Christians?

**Thursday:** *Ps 8: 2, 5-9*
*Lk 24: 35-48 (Jesus appears to his disciples)*

There is little doubt that Jesus' disciples believed that he had been raised from the dead and that they experienced him in a profoundly significant way. In today's reading, Luke tries to express some of the impressions left by the risen Christ on his disciples, but leaves us with as many questions as answers. What was the nature of this risen body, for example? These are questions which we cannot answer. Like the disciples, we are simply invited to accept Jesus as our risen Lord.

- How do you feel about the prospect of your own death? How does belief in the resurrection help you live more fully before death?

- Spend some time hearing Jesus say to you, "Peace be with you!"

**Friday:** *Ps 118: 1-2, 4, 22-27*
        *Jn 21: 1-14 (Appearance by the Sea of*
            *Tiberius)*

This passage is reminiscent of the call of
Simon, Andrew, James and John. Before Jesus
called them to be disciples, they had been
fishermen. Upon finding them fishing out at sea,
the risen Jesus told them to cast out one more
time, and they netted an abundance of fish. Jesus
then nourished them for their new role as fishers
of people.

• How does God's grace nourish you in your
  everyday work? Do you believe your work and
  the successes you've met with were entirely of
  your own doing, or has grace helped you to get
  where you are?

• Do you consider yourself to be a fisher of people? What does this mean to you?

• Pray for the grace to recognize God's hand at
  work in your life.

**Saturday:** *Ps 118: 1, 14-21*
        *Mk 16: 9-15 (Appearances to the faithful)*

This account from Mark seems to summarize
the appearances we have been reflecting upon
this week. Unlike the other passages, however,

we note Jesus reproaching the apostles for their unwillingness to believe what had been told them by Mary and the disciples returning from Emmaus. The Good News comes to us from the words of these first evangelists and we, too, are invited to believe on their words.

• The resurrection of Jesus cannot be proven or disproven. Rather, we are invited to believe on the testimony of those who experienced him, then shared this experience with others. How do you feel about this dynamic? Is it easy for you to believe on the word of others?

• What kind of experience or information would make it easier for you to believe in the resurrection?

# Second Week of Easter

**Monday:** *Ps 2: 1-9*
   *Jn 3: 1-8 (Jesus and Nicodemus)*

The dialogue between Jesus and Nicodemus gives us some ideas concerning the new life that comes to us through the risen Christ. Nicodemus had come to Jesus by night for fear of the Jews and he expressed a very tentative faith in him. Jesus replied by inviting a renewal of identity through baptism and the Holy Spirit.

- What does the phrase, "born of the Spirit," mean to you? Do you consider yourself to be one who has been born of the Spirit?

- What holds you back from completely giving your life over to Jesus?

**Tuesday:** *Ps 93: 1-2, 5*
   *Jn 3: 7-15 (Jesus the revealer of God)*

In today's reading, John proposes that we accept Jesus as the one who reveals to us what we need to know about God. Human reason is confined to knowledge of this world, Jesus tells Nicodemus. Knowledge of God must come from one who is of God. Faith in Jesus lets us share in this knowledge.

- Do you believe that the truths of divine revelation conflict in any way with what human reason can demonstrate to be truth? If so, what are you doing to clarify your thinking?

110

- What did Jesus reveal to us about God that is most important to you? Spend some time thanking God for this gift.

**Wednesday:** *Ps 34: 2-9*
   *Jn 3: 16-21 (Jesus sent to save, not judge)*

Many people believe that God's judgment works as a positive endorsement for, or negative decision against us. Jesus' teaching about light and darkness reminds us that judgment means that God will simply honor those choices we have made in freedom. Those who reject Jesus and the way to God he reveals will be allowed to experience the darkness of soul they have chosen instead. God leaves us free to respond to his love, or to reject him. Were this not the case, we could not share in God's love.

- Verse 20 implies that those who hate the light are ashamed and are afraid to change. Is there anything from your past that you are ashamed of and believe that God has not forgiven? Ask for forgiveness.

- Is it easy for you to change attitudes and behaviors that conflict with the way of love? Pray for the grace to change as love requires.

**Thursday:** *Ps 34: 2, 9, 17-20*
   *Jn 3: 31-36 (Jesus is Lord of all)*

John does not mince words in proclaiming Jesus to be formed from above (i.e., God). He does not see in Jesus merely an enlightened or wise man, still less a prophet. Jesus is one who speaks God's own words, and our response to him should be one of reverent obedience.

- Many saints said that obedience to Jesus allowed them their deepest experience of freedom. Do you experience the truth of this paradox in your own life?

- In what area of your life are you most obedient to Jesus? Most disobedient?

- Pray for the grace to allow Jesus to be Lord of your life.

**Friday:** *Ps 27: 1, 4, 13-14*
   *Jn 6: 1-15 (Miracle of the loaves)*
   This account of the feeding of the multitude is common to all four gospels and represents one of the strongest of traditions. Most theologians see in this miracle a connection with the belief in Jesus as the Bread of Life, who fills all our hungers.

- Jesus blessed the little that was offered in a spirit of sharing. Do you believe that your gifts of time, talent and money offered in love are blessed by God? How do you experience this blessing?

- What can you offer to share with others today in a spirit of love? Ask God to bless your offering.

**Saturday:** *Ps 33: 1-2, 4-5, 18-19*
*Jn 6: 16-21 (Jesus walks on water)*

Today's reading is yet another example of an incident presented by the evangelist to appeal to faith, and not to invite skepticism. Regardless of what really happened, the meaning of Jesus' walk on the water is to be found in his rejoining his disciples. It is a reminder to us, too, that nothing can separate us from the love of the risen Christ.

- What are the primary causes of stress and anxiety in your life? What lifestyle alterations can you make to eliminate some of the more destructive causes of stress?

- Let your imagination create a sea filled with your usual sources of stress and needless anxiety. Invite Jesus to walk over these troubled waters in your mind. Hear him saying, "It is I. Do not be afraid."

# Third Week of Easter

**Monday:** *Ps 119: 23-30*
        *Jn 6: 22-29 (The people seek their king)*

Jesus had fed the crowds, and they were eager to make him king. Knowing this, he fled from their midst and joined his disciples in their boat. The crowd sought him out, for anyone who could feed multitudes by blessing a few crumbs could solve all logistical problems involved in making war against the Romans. Jesus corrected their misconception about him by inviting them to work for the kind of food that will last.

• Are you looking for Jesus? Where, and how do you think Jesus is to be found?

• Pray for the grace to hunger for the things of God.

**Tuesday:** *Ps 31: 3-4, 6-8, 17, 21*
        *Jn 6: 30-35 (Jesus, the Bread of Life)*

One of the ways in which the evangelists tried to convert Jews was by explaining how Jesus fulfilled the prophecies of old. In today's reading, John has Jesus pointing out that the manna which the Jews ate in the desert was only a symbol for the Bread which satisfies all hungers.

• What kind of works of yours are signs to others that you are a follower of Jesus Christ?

• Spend some time letting God love you and satisfy your spiritual hungers.

**Wednesday:** *Ps 66: 1-7*
      *Jn 6: 35-40 (We shall be raised up)*

Today's reading teaches us a tremendous lesson. Jesus' resurrection demonstrated the power of God over the forces of evil, and guaranteed that those who are with Jesus shall themselves be raised up. This will be true for us so long as we strive to do the will of the one who has sent Jesus.

- Grace refers to all those unearned blessings that have helped to make us who we are. Reflect on some of the graces from your early life and family that helped form you (parents, teachers, place of birth, etc.). List these in your journal and give thanks to God for them.

- Spend some time with the passage, "I have come not to do my own will, but the will of him who sent me."

**Thursday:** *Ps 66: 8-9, 16-17, 20*
      *Jn 6: 44-51 (Jesus, the Living Bread)*

The Jews complained that Jesus could not be from God since they knew of his earthly origins. Jesus replied that there was a spiritual side to him that was of God, and if they wanted to know about God, they had only to look to him.

- What are some of the sources of grace in your life now? How do these gifts help to make you who you are?

- Think of some way to let the people who are grace to you know that you are thankful for the gifts they bring to your life.

**Friday:** *Ps 117: 1, 2*
       *Jn 6: 52-59 (More on the Bread of Life)*

These are some of the most uncompromising words ever attributed to Jesus. The Greek word for flesh used by John refers to bodily flesh, causing us to ask, with the Jews, "How can this man give us his flesh to eat?" This unmistakable allusion to the importance of the Eucharist should remind us that Jesus' gift of his life is the greatest gift we can receive.

- Many people who proclaim Jesus as their Lord and Savior speak of him as having died for their sins. How do you understand this? How has Jesus given his life for you?

- List a few of the many changes that have come to the world because of Jesus. Spend some time thanking God for these graces which determine the social and cultural contexts for our lives.

**Saturday:** *Ps 116: 12-17*
         *Jn 6: 60-69 (Spirit and life)*

John finally concludes his reflection on the Bread of Life by pointing out that the truly important aspect of Jesus' teaching is that it reveals to us what is spirit and life. Many of Jesus' followers could not accept his teachings, and so they left him. When confronted with this choice, the apostles, with Peter as their spokesman, proclaimed their faith in Jesus.

- What teachings about Jesus or other church teachings do you find "hard to endure"? What are you doing to help clarify your understanding of this doctrine?

- Many people forsake Jesus and his way every day. Hear him asking you, "Do you want to leave me too?" Give him your response.

# Fourth Week of Easter

**Monday:** *Ps 42: 2-3; 43: 3-4*
*Jn 10: 1-10 (The Good Shepherd)*

Jesus used many examples to explain the relationship between God and people. In today's reading, John recalls Jesus identifying himself as the sheepgate. Out in the fields, sheep were herded into corrals, and shepherds lay in the openings of the corrals when they slept in order to protect the sheep. So, too, has Jesus laid down his life for us.

- Do you believe the following of Jesus will enable you to experience life to the full? What is the full life?

- Spend some time reflecting on Jesus' promise to be committed to our growth and development. How does this make you feel?

**Tuesday:** *Ps 87: 1-7*
*Jn 10: 22-30 (Jesus is one with the Father)*

Today's reading brings to mind a saying by C. S. Lewis, who maintained that a man who said and did the things Jesus said and did was either who he said he was or else he was a lunatic on the level of a poached egg. There is truly no middle ground left to the interpreter of the meaning of Jesus' life; he did not intend there to be.

- Who are the "sheep" whose well-being the Father has entrusted to you? Have you been faithful to them lately? How can you better love them?

- Pray for the grace to be more loving toward family members.

**Wednesday:** *Ps 67: 2-3, 5, 6, 8*
  *Jn 12: 44-50 (Jesus' word shall judge)*

The resurrection signified that God had set his seal on Jesus, that his claims are true, and that his teachings are authoritative. When confronted with the words of Jesus, our response is our judgment, for to refuse to live according to his way is to be cut off from the fullness of life he offers. Yet if we choose to accept him, we shall experience eternal life—life with God.

- How do you feel about non-Christians? Do you believe they can attain salvation? Do you feel any special obligation to "enlighten" them?

- Pray for those people in your life who need to know Jesus in a more personal way.

**Thursday:** *Ps 89: 2-3, 21-22, 25, 27*
  *Jn 13: 16-20 (Jesus, the servant)*

Jesus' resurrection won for us the grace to love as God loves. This love is to take the form of loving service, however, and is not to be used for self-glorification.

- Leo Tolstoy wrote that people who live according to principles other than love can justify all sorts of treachery against other people and invoke their principle as a rationale. Do you believe this?

- Who are the primary beneficiaries of the loving service you offer? Can you expand this circle?

**Friday:** *Ps 2: 6-11*
> *Jn 14: 1-6 (Jesus is the way, the truth, the life)*

In today's reading, Christian beliefs concerning Jesus are focused beautifully by John. Jesus is the firstborn of the new creation and he has gone to prepare a place for us. He has revealed to us the way, the truth, and the life that will bring us to unity with him and one another.

- Meditate on several words/phrases that express your understanding/experience of Jesus as the way, the truth, and the life.

- Does your belief in life after death empower you to live more fully now, or does it cause you to procrastinate your life away?

**Saturday:** *Ps 98: 1-4*
> *Jn 14: 7-14 (The great works to come)*

During his earthly ministry, Jesus offered many awe-inspiring examples of the Father's care for us. Freed from the constraints of space and time, the risen Jesus can now continue his ministry of building the kingdom of God through each of us. For the grace to help build this kingdom of love and justice, we need only ask.

- Who are the people who minister to your needs on a regular basis? Thank God for them, for they are grace in your life. Think of a creative way to let them know you appreciate them.

- Do you believe that God answers prayer? For what is it appropriate to ask? What does God really want to give us?

- Spend some time with the verse, "Whoever sees me sees the Father." How true is this of you, your identity and your works?

# Fifth Week of Easter

**Monday:** *Ps 115: 1-4, 15-16*
*Jn 14: 21-26 (God dwells within us)*

Today's reading reminds us that there is much about us that is mystery. Truly, we can never really understand ourselves, for there are depths in each of us that only God can plumb. God alone knows the truth about us, so we should be slow to judge ourselves or, worse, to take a false pride in ourselves and our accomplishments.

- How do you understand the verse, "I too will love him and reveal myself to him"? How does God reveal himself to you?

- Do you believe that you know yourself? Is there a sense of mystery you have toward yourself?

- Spend time thanking God for the miracle that you are.

**Tuesday:** *Ps 145: 1-13, 21*
*Jn 14: 27-31 (His peace he leaves us)*

The kind of peace Jesus promises is summed up in the word *shalom*, which means the fullness of life. Although many philosophies and value systems promise this kind of peace, Jesus alone seems to be able to help us experience it consistently.

- Would you describe your usual state of mind as being one of peace? Why? (Why not?) What kinds of situations rob you of peace? When do you usually feel most at peace?

- Pray for the grace to accept the peace which Christ promised.

**Wednesday:** *Ps 122: 1-5*
   *Jn 15: 1-8 (Jesus, the true vine)*

The parable of the vine and the vinegrower expresses the nature of our relationship with God and one another. Like branches, we are dependent on the vine for life and nourishment. If we are not pruned, or disciplined, we shall grow into dissipation, just as unpruned vines do.

- Do you really believe that apart from God you can do nothing meaningful?

- How do you experience the trimming and pruning described in the parable? Does this help you to grow?

- Spend time thanking God for the growth you are experiencing at this time in your life.

**Thursday:** *Ps 96: 1-3, 10*
   *Jn 15: 9-11 (Jesus completes our joy)*

In today's reading, John explains the reason why Jesus came: to invite us to share in God's own joy. There is always something a bit hollow and transient in even our most intense experiences of human pleasure and happiness. Living in love as Christ invites us will increase our human joys and complete them.

- Spend some time with the verse, "As the Father has loved me, so have I loved you."

- Would you describe yourself as a joyful person? Do you know any joyful people? Why are they joyful?

- Pray for the grace to be open to joy.

**Friday:** *Ps 57: 8-12*
    *Jn 15: 12-17 (Love one another)*

Thousands of pages of reflection have been written about Jesus Christ and the meaning of his revelation for us. Jesus sums it all up in today's reading—briefly! We are to bear fruit for the glory of God, for God has chosen us to share with each other his love for us.

- A pious tradition has it that at the end of our lives, when we stand before God, he will ask us but one question: "Have you lived your life in such a way as to show others that I loved you?" How would you answer regarding this past week?

- Do you believe that God has chosen you to be one of his friends? How do you experience this?

**Saturday:** *Ps 100: 1-3, 5*
    *Jn 15: 18-21 (The persecutions to come)*

Jesus did not delude his followers with promises of a pain-free, "pie-in-the-sky" life experience. He experienced resistance and constant attack during his earthly ministry, and he warned us that we should not expect better treatment from those in darkness.

- Faulkner wrote that if he had to choose between experiencing pain and experiencing nothing, he would always choose pain. How about you? How does your attempt to follow Jesus cause you pain?

- Pray for the grace to find meaning in your experiences of pain.

# Sixth Week of Easter

**Monday:** *Ps 149: 1-6, 9*
*Jn 15: 26-16: 4 (We must bear witness)*

With the resurrection came a mandate to spread the news of the forgiveness of sin and victory over death which Christ brought. To help us in this endeavor, God's own Spirit—the Spirit who raised Jesus from the dead—will be our helper.

- How do you feel about sharing your religious beliefs with family members? With friends? With working acquaintances?

- What are some of the key issues facing your local secular community? How are you involved in helping to work through these issues?

- Pray for a filling of the Holy Spirit. (Do this with family and/or friends, if possible.)

**Tuesday:** *Ps 138: 1-3, 7-8*
*Jn 16: 5-11 (The promise of the Spirit)*

In some wonderful and mysterious way, Jesus' life, death and resurrection made it possible for us to enjoy a fuller relationship with God than had been the case prior to his coming. John emphasizes this point today with Jesus telling his disciples that his going will be for their own good.

- Eugene Kennedy wrote that we do not become truly human until we grow close enough to others to be missed. This is what the disciples of Jesus felt when he bade them farewell. Do you enjoy this kind of closeness with anyone? Would anyone miss you if you were to die?

- Pray for the well-being of those special people in your life.

**Wednesday:** *Ps 148: 1-2, 11-14*
       *Jn 16: 12-15 (The Spirit will guide us)*

The church's understanding of the meaning of Jesus has grown quite considerably since John wrote his gospel, although new truths concerning Jesus have not been revealed. Today's reading also hints at the unity of truth in the Spirit who leads us to all truth, religious and otherwise.

- What are you doing to further the development of your mind? Your knowledge of the scriptures? How is this helpful to you?

- What kind of knowledge scares you? Why?

- Pray for the grace to find God in all truth.

**Thursday:** Ascension.

**Friday:** *Ps 47: 2-7*
       *Jn 16: 20-23 (Our hearts will rejoice)*

The disciples of Jesus loved him dearly and

were upset to hear him speak of leaving them.
Jesus likened their sorrow to that of a woman in
labor, suffering now, but rejoicing when her
child is born. So shall it be with those who long
for the things of God.

- Gibran wrote: "Your joy is your sorrow un-
  masked. . . . The deeper that sorrow carves into your being, the more joy you can contain."
  Has this been your experience?

- What/who has brought you your greatest joys?
  What sorrows have accompanied these experiences?

**Saturday:** *Ps 47: 2-3, 8-10*
      *Jn 16: 23-28 (Ask, and you shall receive)*

Many times in scripture we read of asking or
speaking in someone's name. In Jewish culture,
this was tantamount to invoking the authority of
the person whose name was being used in order
to influence the one spoken to. When Jesus urges
us to plead with the Father for things we need in
his name, he is telling us that we, too, may now
enjoy the same graces from God that he experienced. This is indeed joyful news.

- How do you feel about asking for favors from
  God? Why?

- Is it easy for you to articulate your needs to
  others? What kinds of needs do you find it
  hardest to request help in fulfilling? Why?

- Pray for the grace to accept your limitations.

# Seventh Week of Easter

**Monday:** *Ps 68: 2-7*
*Jn 16: 29-33 (The apostles' desertion prophesied)*

Many times Jesus' disciples struggled to comprehend the meaning of his words. When, at the last supper, they believed that they finally understood him, Jesus saw through the shallowness of their comprehension. Faith in him without acceptance of the suffering that will accompany faith has been a problem for Christians from the first.

• What are some of the more urgent issues facing the Christian community of which you are a part? How are you struggling to help work through these issues?

• Spend some time with the verse, "I have told you all this so that you may find peace in me." Allow that peace to pervade your being.

**Tuesday:** *Ps 68: 10-11, 20-21*
*Jn 17: 1-11 (Jesus prays to the Father)*

For the next few days we shall be reflecting on the long, beautiful prayer of Jesus as he anticipates his hour of passion and glory. Through this prayer, John continues to teach us the nature of the relationship between Jesus, the Father, and humanity.

- How is Christ glorified in humanity? How is he glorified in your life?

- St. Ignatius of Loyola had as his goal to do all for the greater honor and glory of God. What do you think of this goal? Is this your goal?

**Wednesday:** *Ps 68: 29-30, 33-36*
    *Jn 17: 11-19 (Jesus consecrated for us)*

It is the work of love to unify people in a dynamic relationship of growth and development. In today's reading, Jesus prays that we might be united with the Father in truth, and he offers the gift of his life to make this unity possible. This is the supreme act of love.

- How does the world hate you for your fidelity to God's commandments? What do you think Jesus means by this?

- Hear the words of the Psalmist describing the love of God: "I have loved you with an everlasting love; I have formed you, and you are mine." Bask in the mystery of this great love.

**Thursday:** *Ps 16: 1-2, 5, 7-11*
    *Jn 17: 20-26 (Jesus prays for us)*

We often forget that Jesus is as concerned about our own walk in faith as he was for his disciples. By writing about this prayer of petition Jesus made in our behalf, John reminds us that Jesus continues to intercede for us before the Father.

- An old saying has it that our problem is not that we are not good, but that we settle for less than the best. Do you believe this? Are you striving to become the best person you can be? Are you satisfied with your present level of spiritual growth?

- Pray for the grace to appreciate God's commitment to loving you.

**Friday:** *Ps 103: 1-2, 11-12, 19-20*
*Jn 21: 15-19 (We now live for God)*

Peter had denied Jesus three times and Jesus knew that he must feel terrible about this. That is why Jesus now gives Peter an opportunity to affirm his love by asking him three times, "Do you love me?" With Peter's affirmative response, Jesus states that acceptance of his love should move us to share our lives with others.

- How does God "put a belt around you and take you where you would rather not go"? What kind of person would you be if you were not committed to following Jesus Christ?

- Hear Jesus asking you, "Do you love me?" After a few minutes, give him your response.

**Saturday:** *Ps 11: 4-5, 7*
*Jn 21: 20-25 (Jesus and John)*

Tradition has it that John the evangelist alone out of all the apostles escaped violent martyrdom. The conversation in today's reading be-

tween Jesus and Peter may well represent an attempt by the evangelist or his own disciples to
correct a belief among the early Christians that
John would not die. The final sentence in this
passage reminds us that the scriptures are not
historical documents in the modern sense, but are
instead the early communities' faith-filled
recollections of the meaning of Jesus' life, death
and resurrection.

- Are you ever envious of those who seem to have
  it better than you? Hear Jesus saying, "What
  does it matter to you (what they have)? You are
  to follow me."

- Pray for the grace to "mind your own business"
  in following Jesus, to quit comparing yourself
  to others.

*Ordinary Time After Pentecost*

# Seventh Week in Ordinary Time

**Monday:** *Ps 93: 1-2, 5*
   *Mk 9: 14-29 (Jesus cures an epileptic)*

The pathology of epilepsy is no longer explained in terms of demonic possession as it was for the people of Jesus' day. Jesus' healing of the epileptic boy was therefore considered an exorcism since medical science did not yet understand this illness. This healing is yet another example of Jesus' desire to make people whole.

• Re-create in imagination the scene between the father and Jesus. Hear Jesus saying, "Everything is possible for anyone who has faith."

• Make a commitment to a day of prayer and fasting for one day this week to deepen your relationship with God and others.

**Tuesday:** *Ps 37: 3-4, 18-19, 27-28, 30-40*
   *Mk 9: 30-37 (On true greatness)*

Jesus continually tried to tell his disciples that their understanding of the Messiah must include suffering and service. In today's reading, he counters their notions of esteem by lauding the simplicity of a child.

• What does greatness mean to you? What would you have to accomplish to consider yourself great?

135

- What does Jesus with the child tell us about God's standards of greatness?

- Pray for the grace of humility.

**Wednesday:** *Ps 119: 165, 168, 171-172, 174-175*
*Mk 9: 38-40 (The name of Jesus)*

In biblical times, names were considered important because they gave identity and a claim upon a person. Using the name of Jesus to exorcise a demon meant calling on the Power whom Jesus invoked in healing.

- How do you feel when other people speak about their relationship with God in a way that seems strange to you? Are you tolerant of them?

- What does it mean to be against Jesus? What are some manifestations of this?

**Thursday:** *Ps 1: 1-4, 6*
*Mk 9: 41-50 (Commitment and responsibility)*

The gospels show Jesus most infuriated at those in leadership positions—parents, teachers and ministers—who lead the naive and ignorant astray for self-serving reasons. Today's reading expresses the seriousness of Christian responsibility.

• Were you ever scandalized by some adult's behavior when you were younger? How did you handle it at the time? How has this affected you?

• Pray for the grace to have "salt in yourself," to know that you are loved by God.

**Friday:** *Ps 119: 12, 16, 18, 27, 34-35*
*Mk 10: 1-12 (On marriage and divorce)*

In a culture that permitted a man to leave his wife for the slightest excuse (but not vice versa), Jesus' words on the seriousness of the marriage commitment were ill-received. He believed, however, that love relationships could not grow without commitment. These words shall forever be challenging.

• What is the value of commitment in a love relationship? Do you believe that God is committed to you?

• Spend time thanking God for those people in your life who are committed to loving you.

**Saturday:** *Ps 103: 13-18*
*Mk 10: 13-16 (Jesus and the children)*

In the non-Jewish communities to whom Mark wrote, children were not recognized as persons with rights. They were often beaten and neglected; infanticide was not uncommon; abor-

tion was accepted. Jesus' love of children
challenged these attitudes and revealed
something very special about God.

• What does it mean to you to accept God's
  kingdom like a little child? Does this describe
  your attitude?

• What are you doing to help alleviate the suffering of children in poor and oppressed countries?

# Eighth Week in Ordinary Time

**Monday:** *Ps 32: 1-2, 5-7*
     *Mk 10: 17-27 (The danger of riches)*

It is noteworthy that Jesus never condemned material goods—not even money and alcohol. His confrontation with the rich young man warns us, however, that the love of material goods can keep us from growing spiritually.

- Let your imagination re-create this encounter between Jesus and the rich young man. See Jesus looking at him in love; hear him challenge the young man to poverty and freedom; note how the young man's face grows sad.

- Why did Jesus challenge the rich young man to give away his goods? Do you believe everyone is called to do this? How about you?

- Pray for the grace to be less attached to material goods.


**Tuesday:** *Ps 50: 5-8, 14, 23*
     *Mk 10: 28-31 (The last shall be first)*

Many people today believe that the rewards for being a follower of Jesus are reserved for the next life. But Jesus also promises that following him will bring blessings in this life as well, though not without suffering.

- Do you believe that the following of Jesus Christ is the best way to live this life? Why? (Why not?)

- What are some of the rewards you experience from following Jesus? What are some of the sufferings?

- Thank God for the gift of life.


**Wednesday:** *Ps 79: 8-9, 11, 13*
         *Mk 10: 32-45 (On servant leadership)*

Mark again contrasts Jesus' notion of the Messiah as a suffering servant with the apostles' ambitions and vanities. Jesus explains that a commitment to service is the only way to guarantee that leadership does not go to one's head.

- Many have written that the proper attitude for a Christian is expressed thus: "What can I do to help?" Do you agree? Does this saying summarize your attitude toward others and circumstances?

- Review your day to come and anticipate times when you will need grace to be more loving. Ask for this grace.


**Thursday:** *Ps 33: 2-9*
        *Mk 10: 46-52 (Bold faith and prayer)*

Time and again Jesus altered his plans to attend to someone in need. In today's reading, we see him restoring sight to a blind man—one who lived by begging. Bartimaeus, the blind man, shows us the value of boldly asking for grace.

• Spend some time with the verse, "What do you want me to do for you?" What is your reply?

• Pray for a deepening in faith.

**Friday:** *Ps 149: 1-6, 9*
         *Mk 11: 11-26 (The withered fig tree)*

Old Testament prophets sometimes compared the people of Israel to trees, branches and vines. Today's stories of the withered fig tree and the cleansing of the Temple show Jesus confronting the barrenness of the Jews of his day for their failure to receive his teaching and their failure to understand the meaning of true worship.

• How do you feel about Jesus' actions in this passage? Is it possible for anger to serve love?

• What kind of activity has been going on in the temple of your soul during the past day?

**Saturday:** *Ps 19: 8-11*
           *Mk 11: 27-33 (The authority of Jesus)*

Jesus' cleansing of the Temple was daring and provocative. When a deputation came up to trap him by asking for his credentials for doing what he had done, Jesus saw through their trap. He sidestepped their charges of blasphemy and arrogance by exposing their complicities concerning John the Baptist.

- Have you ever compromised your perception of truth because you were fearful of others' opinions? Have you done so recently?

- Preview your day and anticipate a time when you will have occasion to say or do something to further Christian truth. Resolve to do something when that time comes.

- Pray for the grace to speak the truth in love.

# Ninth Week in Ordinary Time

**Monday:** *Ps 112: 1-6*
   *Mk 12: 1-12 (Malice in the vineyard)*

The parables of Jesus are symbolic statements about life designed to hold a mirror before us that we might see who we are before God. In today's reading, Jesus describes Israel as a vineyard entrusted to tenants, i.e., to the religious leaders. These leaders killed or mistreated all who were sent to them by God, the owner of the vineyard. Still, Jesus promises, their wickedness will not prevail.

• What kind of steward are you in taking care of the people God has entrusted to you? For the environment? For the government?

• Sketch out a Christ-cornerstone, and lay additional stones representing your gifts on top of it, fashioning a building of some sort.

• Pray for the grace to become a good steward of creation.

**Tuesday:** *Ps 112: 1-2, 7-9*
   *Mk 12: 13-17 (God and Caesar)*

Today's reading describes another important confrontation between Jesus and the authorities. They tried to trap him by baiting him with tax resistance and secular alternatives, either of which would have damaged his influence. He saw through their maliciousness, however, and distinguished between religious and secular responsibilities.

* Are you a good citizen? Do you participate in the political process at least by voting?

* When would it be appropriate for a Christian to disobey governmental authorities?

**Wednesday:** *Ps 25: 2-9*
      *Mk 12: 18-27 (The life to come)*

The Sadducees were a small but powerful group of Jewish religious leaders. They rejected all traditions except those articulated in the Pentateuch, the first five books of the Bible, which give no hint of the immortal nature of the human spirit. Today's reading describes a trap set for Jesus by the Sadducees. Jesus tells them that their God is too small.

* What do you believe heaven is like? Is your idea of heaven merely an image of your own notions of Utopia?

* "Heaven begins on earth, or it does not begin at all," wrote Louis Evely. Do you believe this?

* Pray for the grace to love God above all things.

**Thursday:** *Ps 128: 1-5*
      *Mk 12: 28-34 (The two great
         commandments)*

The two great religious questions are: What kind of God is God, and what does God expect of human beings? Jesus answers both of these questions in today's reading by emphasizing the importance of love.

- Write a short statement about what it means to love God with all your heart, soul, mind and strength. Do these reflections describe your love of God?

- St. Augustine maintained that the love and praise of God was the greatest joy that a human being could experience. Do you agree?

- Pray for the grace to love God more deeply.

**Friday:** *Ps 146: 2, 7-10*
*Mk 12: 35-37 (David's Lord)*

This is a difficult passage. Confronted by the Jews with numerous preconceptions as to what the Messiah would be like, Jesus tried to open their minds to new possibilities. The Messiah would be far more than a blood descendant of David, Jesus assured them. He would be one whom even David would worship.

- What are some misconceptions you have about God that need to be changed? Perhaps the way you complete the following sentences will help you identify these notions.

a. God can't love me; I'm too . . .

b. I can't know God; God is too . . .

c. I can't believe in Jesus; he's too . . .

- Pray for the grace to be more open to God's forgiveness and love for you.

**Saturday:** *Tb 13: 2, 6-8*
        *Mk 12: 38-44 (The widow's mite)*

God will not judge us according to human standards, but according to what we've done with what we've been given. In today's reading, a poor widow is held out by Jesus as an example of true generosity.

- Are you a generous person? Do you give more out of excess than want?

- It has often been said that Christian giving — of money, services, etc. — ought to hurt the giver a little. Do you agree?

# Tenth Week in Ordinary Time

**Monday:** *Ps 34: 2-9*
*Mt 5: 1-12 (The beatitudes)*

As we begin our 12-week reflection on the gospel of Matthew, we hear the beatitudes, a collection of promises extended to the lowly, the humble and the just. "You are blest," Christ promises us. We need only claim our blessings.

- With which of the beatitudes do you identify most closely? Which do you relate to least? How so?

- Spend some time thanking God for his blessings.

**Tuesday:** *Ps 119: 129-133, 135*
*Mt 5: 13-16 (Shining lights)*

Jesus is the new Moses. In depicting Jesus as the one who fulfilled the promises and prophecies of the Old Testament, Matthew gathers the teachings of Jesus and presents them in what is now called the Sermon on the Mount. Just as Moses ascended the mountain and returned with life-giving teachings, so too does Jesus.

- "If you don't love yourself, it will be difficult for you to love others," goes an old saying. Do you agree?

- What do you like most about yourself? What do you like least? How do these dislikes keep your "light under a bushel basket"?

- Pray for the grace to love yourself as God loves you.

**Wednesday:** *Ps 99: 5-9*
   *Mt 5: 17-19 (Jesus and the Law)*

Today's reading summarizes much of what the gospel of Matthew is attempting to articulate: Jesus is the fulfillment of Jewish expectations. Matthew constantly affirms the value of Jewish tradition, and portrays Jesus as one who loved, rather than despised, Judaism.

- How do we teach each other to respect (or despise) the laws of God? What are you a model of most in your family? At work?

- Who are the models you look to for inspiration in living out your faith? What is it about these people that inspires you?

**Thursday:** *Ps 85: 9-14*
   *Mt 5: 20-26 (On anger and reconciliation)*

Jesus looked deeper than human behavior to identify sources of goodness and sin. Behavior follows state of being, he taught; actions are always preceded by thoughts about the actions. If we would transform our angry selves, we must therefore begin to think peaceful thoughts, and we must reconcile with our enemies.

- C. S. Lewis wrote that the Nazis hated the Jews and so they mistreated them, but after awhile they hated them because they mistreated them. Are there people in your life who suffer the same lot from you?

- What are some occasions of anger for you? What do you usually do with your anger? How can you change your thinking about these occasions to lessen your anger?

- Pray for the grace to be more patient with other people.

**Friday:** *Ps 116: 10-11, 15-18*
      *Mt 5: 27-32 (Sexual responsibility)*

The reproductive instinct is one of the strongest of human passions, and one of the most difficult to control. Jesus tells us that the key to responsible sexual expression lies in the way we think about people of the opposite sex. Do we allow ourselves to fantasize adulterous thoughts? If so, then we are in violation of God's law, which has it that responsible sexual expression should take place in the context of a committed relationship.

- How do you view people of the opposite sex? Is it difficult for you to be friends with them? Are many of them friends with you?

- How do you feel about Jesus' teaching on adultery?

**Saturday:** *Ps 103: 1-4, 8-12*
     *Mt 5: 33-37 (Integrity and sincerity)*

The name of God was considered sacred to Jews; indeed, it was forbidden that it be spoken except in reverence. Moses had taught that the name of God should never be spoken in vain, and Jesus stated further that a simple "Yes" or "No" should suffice for occasions when people are prone to swear.

- Are you prone to exaggerate events (especially in your behalf) or twist the truth from time to time to impress others?

- How do you feel about people who curse regularly? Is this a harmless habit, or does it attract stormy thoughts that lead to angry behavior?

- Spend some time reverencing the name of Yahweh, "I Am Who Am."

# Eleventh Week in Ordinary Time

**Monday:** *Ps 98: 1-4*
  *Mt 5: 38-42 (Nonviolent resistance)*

Today's reading addresses the issue of breaking the cycle of violence. Because violence bequeaths violence, Jesus commanded his followers to refuse to perpetuate this cycle. Nonviolent resistance, he believed, was the best way to convert the violent of this world.

- "An eye for an eye is making the world blind," said Gandhi. Do you agree? Do you believe Jesus commanded us to refuse to stand up to evil? How should a Christian respond to evil?

**Tuesday:** *Ps 146: 2, 5-9*
  *Mt 5: 43-48 (Love your enemies)*

Jesus' command to love our enemies is one of the most unique of all his teachings. Because all people are children of God, we ought to love them all—even those with whom we disagree. Then will new things happen in our lives and in our world.

- Is it possible to disagree with someone and still love that person? Think of a few people with whom you often disagree; how can you love them?

- Do you believe it is ever appropriate for a Christian to kill someone with whom he or she disagrees?

- Pray for the grace to be able to recognize all people as children of God.

**Wednesday:** *Ps 112: 1-4, 9*
       *Mt 6: 1-6, 16-18 (Purity of heart)*

Motives are important, Jesus taught. People who are motivated by others' opinions are sure to fall short of that single-hearted love of God that Jesus calls us to. External motivations regarding charity and prayer can especially frustrate spiritual growth.

- Why do you pray? How important to you is it that others know you pray?

- Think of something nice you can do for someone today without the person even knowing that you did it.

**Thursday:** *Ps 111: 1-4, 7-8*
       *Mt 6: 7-15 (The Lord's Prayer)*

Today's reading emphasizes the importance of being sincere and honest with God. Because God is not impressed by the length of time that we pray, or how many words we say, or how much we promise to give him, Jesus shares with us a formula for prayer that plugs us into grace and forgiveness.

- With each verse of the Lord's Prayer, spend some time reflecting on how your own life is addressed by these words. Add your own reflections.

- What faults in other people bother you most? How are these faults made manifest in your own life? Ask God for forgiveness.

**Friday:** *Ps 34: 2-7*
  *Mt 6: 19-23 (Heavenly treasure)*

Again we return to the issue of motives. The philosopher Durant wrote that we do not desire that which we find reasonable, but we find reasons for that which we desire. Ignatius of Loyola stated that our motives were either toward love or selfishness. We had best check ourselves often.

- What do you treasure most in this world? How does your heart serve this treasure?

- Look back over the key events of the past day. What were your motives for saying and doing what you did?

- Pray for the grace to be motivated by love.

**Saturday:** *Ps 34: 8-13*
  *Mt 6: 24-34 (Trust in God)*

This is one of the most cherished of all of Jesus' teachings. For those who treasure God's will above all else, he promises freedom from worry and peace of mind.

- What/whom do you worry about most often? What can you do to lessen your worries? How can you let go of unreasonable causes of worry?

- Because worry is usually directed toward future events that we can do nothing about in the present, resolve to try to spend more time in the present moment today. Begin now. Whenever worry arises, direct your attention back to the present, which is the only moment that exists.

# Twelfth Week in Ordinary Time

**Monday:** *Ps 33: 12-13, 18-22*
   *Mt 7: 1-5 (Do not judge)*

Christianity is a religion that emphasizes full, deep, intimate relationships between people. Because our judgments against other people limit our relationships with them, Jesus told us to suspend judgment until we are perfect. For most of us, that will take forever.

- An old saying goes, "Search for the perfect church, and if you find it, join it. But know that as soon as you join it, it will have ceased to be the perfect church." What do you hold against your church? Why?

- Which family members have you judged most harshly? Pray for the grace to forgive yourself and them, and resolve to start anew in your relationship with them.

**Tuesday,** *Ps 15: 2-5*
   *Mt 7: 6, 12-14 (The narrow gate)*

Today's reading includes three loosely related teachings. In striving to walk the difficult path of love, we are warned that we should not profane sacred truths and rituals by sharing them with people who cannot receive them or are not ready to. This caution does not mean that we should become exclusive or elitist, however.

- What is the golden rule that sums up your philosophy about relationships with other people? How is this different from verse 12?

- With what kind of people do you find it most difficult to share your beliefs about Christ? How do you relate with these people?

**Wednesday:** *Ps 105: 1-9*
        *Mt 7: 15-20 (By their fruits . . .)*

Now we come to the criterion for discerning truth: Examine the "fruits." Where the fruits of self-indulgence (see Gal 5: 19-21) abound in a person's life, be aware of hypocrisy or false teaching. Where the fruits of the Spirit (Gal 5: 22-24) adorn a person's life, listen to what he or she has to say.

- List some of the spiritual fruits that you believe your family members would say characterize you . . . that your co-workers see in you . . . that you would ascribe to yourself.

- Do you know anyone whose life is characterized by the fruits of the Spirit? Resolve to spend more time with this person.

**Thursday:** *Ps 106: 1-5*
        *Mt 7: 21-29 (Build on Jesus)*

We conclude our meditation on the teachings of Christ by listening to Jesus tell us that he wants far more than holy words to characterize our lives. He challenges us to build on the cornerstone he laid by acting in love through the day, each day.

- "Love God, and do as you please," wrote St. Augustine. Do you agree with this statement? Why? (Why not?)

- What are people who do not build their lives on Christ missing? How is this costly to them?

- Pray for the grace to believe more deeply in Jesus Christ.

**Friday:** *Ps 128: 1-5*
    *Mt 8: 1-4 (Jesus heals a leper)*

In many accounts of healings by Jesus, we hear him cautioning those he cured to tell no one. The leper in today's reading was instructed to go to the priests so he might be released from his banishment from society. The injunction to tell no one else reveals Jesus' concern for the proper interpretation of his miracles.

- Do you accept your bodiliness and the strengths and limitations that go with it?

- How do you think other people view your bodily appearance? How much does it matter to you what they think?

- Pray for the grace to be able to accept yourself as you are now.

**Saturday:** *Lk 1: 46-50, 53-55*
     *Mt 8: 5-17 (More healings)*

In the passage describing the cure of the centurion's son, Jesus shows us that he will respond to faith wherever he finds it. By opening himself up to be touched by the pain of others, he was able to offer them healing and wholeness, regardless of their age or creed.

- What are you doing to take care of your body, a temple of the Holy Spirit? Do you ever abuse your body? How can you take better care of your body?

- How willing are you to let other people share their pain with you? How do you decide when it is appropriate to say "No" to them?

# Thirteenth Week in Ordinary Time

**Monday:** *Ps 103: 1-4, 8-11*
  *Mt 8: 18-22 (The cost of discipleship)*

At first glance, Jesus seems to be very hard on those he invited to follow him. This passage, coming after accounts of healing, reveals that Jesus did not want people like the scribe to follow him on the impulse of the moment without counting the cost. The man who wanted to wait until his father was buried was not yet ready to leave home.

- What habit or relationship have you been hanging onto that keeps you from changing as you know you must? Do something today to begin to grow out of this death-dealing security.

- "Today is the first day of the rest of your life," goes an old saying. Spend some time thinking about your day. Resolve to live it fully.

**Tuesday:** *Ps 26: 2-3, 9-12*
  *Mt 8: 23-27 (Jesus calms a storm)*

The Sea of Galilee is a place where storms arise suddenly and violently. Just as quickly, they move along, leaving a calm sea behind them. Most significant in today's reading is not a revelation of Jesus' power over nature, but a promise that if we have faith he can calm the storms in our own lives.

- What are some sources of stress that you encounter regularly? Why do these situations cause you stress? How can you change your attitude about these situations to diminish stress?

- Pray for the grace to be more adaptable in stressful situations.

**Wednesday:** *Ps 34: 7-8, 10-13*
    *Mt 8: 28-34 (Demoniacs and swineherds)*

This is another unusual miracle that is most meaningful when interpreted symbolically. Jesus' expulsion of the demoniacs into the swineherd does not indicate his displeasure over raising hogs (as some have written), but his high evaluation of the worth of human life.

- If you were to suddenly inherit $1,000,000, how would you change your lifestyle? How important is economics in your list of priorities?

- The Gadarenes ordered Jesus out of their district because he was obviously bad for business. Do you believe Jesus is still expelled by business? How so?

**Thursday:** *Ps 116: 1-9*
    *Mt 9: 1-8 (Jesus and the paralytic)*

Today's reading makes little sense unless we realize that Jews believed sickness to be a manifestation of the power of sin in the world. By offering the paralytic forgiveness and healing, Jesus revealed his power over the forces of sin.

- How does sin most often break into your life? Hear Jesus' words, "Have courage, your sins are forgiven." Pray for the grace to accept God's forgiveness.

- Do you know someone who is sick, or feeling depressed, or is overburdened and who would appreciate some kind of support from you?

**Friday:** *Ps 106: 1-5*
*Mt 9: 9-12 (The call of Matthew)*

Matthew never forgot that Jesus had called him out of his position of disrepute and oppression. Whenever he mentions himself, he quickly adds that he was once a tax collector. So, too, do we need to recall how the Lord has lifted us up and helped us to grow.

- "When we remember, we are re-membered," goes a pious saying. Do you take enough time to recall your roots? Resolve to call up a friend and/or family member today to help you appreciate your past. Take out an old photo album to browse through during the course of this week.

- Are you a self-righteous person? How does this show up in your life?

- Pray for the grace to recognize grace in your life.

**Saturday:** *Ps 135: 1-6*
     *Mt 9: 14-17 (Jesus the bridegroom)*

Jesus came to bring a spirit of freshness and vitality among us. But if we are to grow in the Spirit, we must change old, self-centered or out-moded ways of thinking about ourselves and life. If we do not change, the new wine of the Spirit will not remain within us.

• Does the prospect of continuing to grow (change) in Christ frighten you? What are you most reluctant to change? Why?

• Do you believe that the church is open to changing traditions that are outmoded? Why are some people so bothered by this? How important is it to you that the church can be open to changing where necessary?

• Pray for the grace to be willing to change for the sake of Christ.

# Fourteenth Week in Ordinary Time

**Monday:** *Ps 91: 1-4, 14-15*
*Mt 9: 18-26 (Two miraculous cures)*

In today's reading, Jesus restores a young girl to life and heals an elderly woman who had been hemorrhaging for 12 years. During an age when women and children were basically disenfranchised in society, Jesus' treatment of women was quite revolutionary.

• What does our culture hold out as qualities of masculinity and femininity? How do these stereotypes limit male and female self-expression?

• How do you feel about the church's treatment of male and female sexuality? Why?

• Pray for the grace to be more open to the gifts of others.


**Tuesday:** *Ps 17: 1-3, 6-8, 15*
*Mt 9: 32-38 (The harvest is rich)*

Matthew tells us of Jesus healing a mute, who then began to speak. He also encourages us to share Jesus' desire that people become more willing to minister to one another. Let us begin anew today.

• Do you believe there is a crisis in the church as far as ministry is concerned? Why? (Why not?)

• Do you consider yourself to be a minister?

**Wednesday:** *Ps 33: 2-3, 10-11, 18-19*
      *Mt 10: 1-7 (Jesus commissions the Twelve)*

An old saying has it that it is far easier for ten people to do the work of ten than for one person to try to do the work of ten. In choosing and commissioning disciples, Jesus multiplied his influence many times. His Spirit still supports us in this model of ministry.

- Do you feel supported by your community in your ministerial endeavors? Do you need more support? (How could you receive it?)

- Go over the events planned for your day ahead. Against these plans, hear Jesus' words, "The reign of God is at hand." Let these words deepen your anticipation to love this day.

**Thursday:** *Ps 105: 16-21*
      *Mt 10: 7-15 (The command to travel light)*

Jesus sent his disciples out into the towns and countryside with a simple message and a powerful ministry in order to prepare the people for his own visitation. The disciples were told that this task was worthy of room and board, but that there would be those who rejected them. So it is for all trying to be ministers of the gospel.

- Do you do your share to help support people committed to full-time ministry in the church? What do you have to contribute in terms of time, talent and money?

- Spend some time with the passage, "The gifts you have received return as gifts." What are some of your most characteristic gifts? How do you share these with others? What happens to you when you cling to your giftedness?

**Friday:** *Ps 37: 3-4, 18-19, 27-28, 39-40*
　　　*Mt 10: 16-23 (Persecutions to come)*

Because the early church experienced persecution from Jews and gentiles, Jesus' warning in today's reading offered words of consolation and hope. Persecution was to be expected even from family members, Jesus explained, but the consolation of the Spirit would be given to those in need.

- Do you believe that the people of today would crucify Jesus if he were to come among us in person as he did years ago?

- How have you been persecuted for Christ's sake during the past week?

- Pray for the grace of endurance.

**Saturday:** *Ps 105: 1-4, 6-7*
　　　*Mt 10: 24-33 (The value of endurance)*

Matthew offers still more consolation to a persecuted church in today's reading. If people were so callous as to call the Lord of love Beelzebul, what can we expect? he asks us. We should not allow such people to contaminate our souls, however. Endurance will bring us to Christ.

- What does it mean to you to acknowledge Christ before other people? How are you doing this in your life?

- How would you finish this sentence? "I would never deny Christ unless . . ."

- Pray for the grace to know that God is closer to you than your very breath.

# Fifteenth Week in Ordinary Time

**Monday:** *Ps 124: 1-8*
*Mt 10: 34-11:1 (Take up your cross)*

The key to appreciating Jesus' message is to realize that he calls us to become more deeply related to other people. We do this not because they need us, but because we need them to be ourselves. Because our selfishness opposes relationships, we must take up the cross of dying to selfishness.

- How do you feel about the verse, "My mission is to spread not peace, but division"? What does Jesus mean by this?

- Place yourself somewhere on a continuum of attitudes regarding strangers. Strangers are:
  God's Grace _____ Nuisances
  Are you content to stay where you are on this continuum?

- Pray for the grace to be open to the gifts that others bring.

**Tuesday:** *Ps 69: 3, 14, 30-34*
*Mt 11: 20-24 (Woes to towns)*

If we are waiting for a greater gift from God than Jesus, we shall have to wait forever. That is the message Matthew brings to us in today's reading. It was not so much that the people of

Chorazin, Bethsaida and Capernaum rejected Jesus, but that they failed to reform.

- Do you take your nationality for granted? Your faith? Jesus Christ? Spend some time thanking God for these gifts.

- Call to mind someone close to you who has drifted away in intimacy lately. Resolve to do something to bring this relationship closer.

**Wednesday:** *Ps 103: 1-7*
  *Mt 11: 25-27 (Good News for the simple)*

Accepting the Good News of Jesus Christ is not so much a matter of intellectual sophistication, but a matter of faith. In today's reading, Jesus warns us of the danger of intellectual snobbery.

- How do you respond to people who say to you, "How can you believe all that religious stuff? There's no proof for any of it!"?

- Pray for the grace to accept Christ in simplicity of heart.

**Thursday:** *Ps 105: 1, 5, 8-9, 24-27*
  *Mt 11: 28-30 (Burdens removed)*

When we try to live life only out of the capital of our own resources, we are sure to become burdened. Those who embrace Christ's way are promised burdens shared and spiritual refreshment.

- What kind of burdens do you need help shouldering? Tell Jesus all about it, especially articulating your feelings about these burdens. Ask him to let you know that he is with you. Resolve to share these same feelings with a friend whom you trust.

- Spend some time with the verse, "Come to me . . ." Feel God's desire for you.

**Friday:** *Ps 116: 12-18*
     *Mt 12: 1-8 (God wants mercy)*

From this point on in Matthew's gospel, the Jewish authorities begin an open campaign to trap Jesus and discredit his ministry. Jesus does not accept their accusations of disobedience to the Law, however, reminding them that the mercy of God is at the heart of the Law.

- What are some of the key issues facing the church today? What are you doing to inform yourself concerning these issues? How are you expressing your opinions about the church?

- How do you generally react when other people confront you for something you're doing wrong? Why do you respond like this? How can you do better?

**Saturday:** *Ps 136: 1, 23-24, 10-15*
     *Mt 12: 14-21 (Jesus as Isaiah's servant)*

The prophet Isaiah had described a servant

who would be gentle of spirit, but despised by humanity. This mysterious figure was not usually associated with the glorious, kingly messiah expected by the Jews, but Matthew tells us today that it was because our Messiah suffered for us that we can now hope.

• People followed Jesus because he was kind to them, and his kindness aroused affection in them. What do you seek more of from others: affection or admiration (which is somewhat less intimate)? Why?

• Spend some time with the verse, "Here is my servant whom I have chosen, my loved one in whom I delight." Let God delight in you.

# Sixteenth Week in Ordinary Time

**Monday:** *Ex 15: 1-6*
*Mt 12: 38-42 (The sign of Jonah)*

It is doubtful that Jesus could have worked any kind of sign to inspire loving faith in the hearts of those who persecuted him. People who sought truth and who were humble found in him all that they needed.

- Father John Powell wrote that to the people who said to Jesus, "Show us and we will believe," Jesus replied, "Believe, and I will show you." What kind of knowledge does faith make possible?

- What kind of sign of God's presence is needed most in today's world? How can you manifest this sign today?

**Tuesday:** *Ex 15: 8-10, 12, 17*
*Mt 12: 46-50 (The family of Christ)*

"Your children are not your children," wrote Gibran. "They are the sons and daughters of Life's longing for itself." In today's reading, Jesus affirms the primacy of the family of God over blood relations.

- Have you left the home of your youth (emotionally as well as physically)? Are you still living your life according to adolescent patterns?

171

- What kind of regard do you seek from family members? How important is this to you? Why?

- Pray for the grace to see all people as children of God.

**Wednesday:** *Ps 78: 18-19, 23-28*
        *Mt 13: 1-9 (Parable of the sower)*

Jesus revealed to us a God intent on communicating his love and vision. Because Jesus did not want to reach only the intellectuals of his day, he told parables, simple stories, to describe the kingdom of God. Today's parable of the sower and the seed is rich with meaning concerning social development and our own spiritual growth as well.

- What kinds of sentiments have you been spreading at home lately? Pick out one or two people from home and count the number of times you have affirmed them during the past two days. How many times have you criticized them? Resolve to be more loving.

- Spend some time allowing God to work in the soils of your heart.

**Thursday:** *Dn 3: 52-56*
        *Mt 13: 10-17 (More on parables)*

Although the parables are relatively simple stories, they are nonetheless rich in symbolism. In order to appreciate their meaning, we must allow them to confront our lives as a mirror reflects back to us our bodily image. The more time and effort we put into the struggle of meditating on the parables, the greater will be our reward.

- "In the spiritual life, if you're not progressing, you're regressing." Do you agree with this? Why? (Why not?) In what direction have you been making a net advance lately?

- Pray for the grace to hunger for growth.

**Friday:** *Ps 19: 8-11*
*Mt 13: 18-23 (A parable explained)*

Jesus taught his disciples many things that he did not explain to the crowds. He wanted to be certain that they understood his words, for he knew that they would one day have to expound on them. In today's reading, he explains the meaning of the parable of the sower, leaving its symbolism intact while developing its meaning.

- What kinds of seeds have you been sowing at work lately? Pick out a few people with whom you work and examine how you have related with them in the past two days. How often were you critical of them, at least to yourself? Resolve to be more affirming.

- What kinds of things are growing in the good soil of your heart? In the briers? In the rocky ground? Along the path?

**Saturday:** *Ps 50: 1-2, 5-6, 14-15*
*Mt 13: 24-30 (Parable of the weeds and wheat)*

This parable is extremely rich in meaning. The weeds, known as darnel or bastard wheat in some translations, are almost impossible to distinguish from the wheat when both are seedlings. Because God is a wheat grower and not a weed puller, he allows both to grow together.

- "That which seems most feeble and bewildered in you is the strongest and most determined," wrote Gibran. What kind of strength is he talking about here?

- The converse of the above statement might be, "That which you think to be your greatest strength of character is often your downfall." Have you ever experienced this?

# Seventeenth Week
# in Ordinary Time

**Monday:** *Ps 106: 19-23*
       *Mt 13: 31-35 (Parables of growth)*

"Things take time," reads a poster circulated widely today. Jesus would have concurred. Although beginning in relative obscurity, the influence of Christ through his church has been a powerful leaven for good in the world. His influence in our lives can be no less encouraging.

- Are you a better person now than you were six months ago? One year ago? Five years ago? How so?

- Spend some time with this passage from Paul's writings, "Though the outer person is falling into decay, the inner self is renewed day by day."

**Tuesday:** *Ps 103: 6-13*
       *Mt 13: 36-43 (Parable of the weeds explained)*

Again we find Jesus explaining his parables to his disciples, but he invites everyone to be open to his teaching. We live in a world that is both good and bad, Jesus tells us. God can purge the evil from our midst, but we must hear his words of love and put them into practice.

- Some philosophers have argued that goodness is merely the absence of evil; others, notably

St. Augustine, argued that evil is the absence of
good. Where do you stand on the issue of
sources for good and evil?

- How does hearing God's word help you to
  become a better person? Write down your
  thoughts. Spend some time thanking God for
  the gift of the scriptures.

**Wednesday:** *Ps 99: 5-7, 9*
        *Mt 13: 44-46 (The pearl of great price)*

The two mini-parables in today's reading
emphasize the kind of response to Jesus to which
we are called. Like the people in the parables, we
are invited to set his kingdom as our highest
priority, organizing our lives according to God's
will.

- If you could write out a job description explicitly suited for your fullest response to Jesus
  Christ, what would it include (type of work,
  salary, benefits, whom you would work with,
  etc.)? How closely does your present occupation come to this ideal work? How long do you
  intend to remain in your present occupation?

- Pray for the grace to treasure the things of
  God.

**Thursday:** *Ps 84: 3-6, 8, 11*
        *Mt 13: 47-53 (Parable of the dragnet)*

Today's parable teaches us an important

lesson. Jesus came to transform humanity, but he accepted the world in its messiness as well. So too are we invited to accept our messy world and broken lives as worthy of transformation.

- Imagine that God cast a spiritual dragnet into your soul today. What would be dragged out? What would you most like to keep? What do you want to throw away?

- Pray for the grace to know that God loves you just as you are now.

**Friday:** *Ps 81: 3-6, 10-11*
    *Mt 13: 54-58 (His own town rejects Jesus)*

It is ironical that the people we are closest to are also the people who often limit us most. This is what happened to Jesus in Nazareth. His brethren (relatives) were not open to his ministry because their ideas of him were too limited.

- Do you feel that the people you live with love and accept you just as you are? How about the people you work with?

- "We like people in proportion to the good we do them and not in proportion to the good they do us," wrote Laurence Sterne. Do you agree?

**Saturday:** *Ps 67: 2-3, 5, 7-8*
    *Mt 14: 1-12 (John the Baptist beheaded)*

The Navajo Indians believed that conscience was a tiny triangle that turned inside the human heart. When we tended toward immorality, the triangle rubbed the walls of the heart and caused pain, which helped steer us back toward goodness. Some people, however, had become so immoral that the points on the triangle were smoothed out, and they felt nothing in conscience any longer.

- Do you believe that some people are hopelessly wicked?

- Do you believe you have a well-formed conscience? Are you sensitive to your conscience? How do you feel when you behave contrary to your conscience? What do you usually do with these feelings?

# Eighteenth Week in Ordinary Time

**Monday:** *Ps 81: 12-17*
   *Mt 14: 13-21 (Jesus feeds the multitudes)*

Jesus loved John the Baptist very deeply. When he heard of John's death, he sought a lonely place where he could mourn the loss of his friend, but the crowds were to deny him even this small amount of privacy. His response to them was one of mercy, however, and not reproach.

- "My interruptions are my work," wrote Henri Nouwen. How do you handle interruptions? Do you believe that some interruptions are God's way of breaking into your life?

- Think over your day, anticipating times when you will probably get interrupted. How can you respond in love? Pray for the grace to remember to do so when those times come.

**Tuesday:** *Ps 51: 3-7, 12-13*
   *Mt 14: 22-36 (Jesus, the mysterious)*

Today's reading includes many mysterious events ascribed to Jesus. He sends a crowd he has just fed with a miraculous meal back to their homes, then he spends time in prayer; he walks on the water, and people who touch his clothing are healed. Like Peter, however, we are invited only to put our faith and trust in him, even though there are many things about him that we shall never understand.

- What notions about Jesus make it difficult for you to believe and trust in him? To whom can you speak for guidance in working through these blocks to personal growth? Resolve to do so during the coming week.

- Although he had a very busy schedule, Jesus nonetheless found time to pray. How faithful to prayer are you? How important to you is prayer?

**Wednesday:** *Ps 106: 6-7, 13-14, 21-23*
*Mt 15: 21-28 (Messiah of the gentiles)*

This passage describes an event which took place during the only time Jesus ever ventured outside Jewish territory. Seeking to gain a respite from the demands of the crowds who followed him and from the authorities who tormented him, he is confronted by a persistent Canaanite woman. Even though she was a gentile and, as a Canaanite, a member of the Jews' most ancient enemies, her faith and love finally moved Jesus to grant her requests.

- "The family that prays together, stays together," is a familiar saying. How important is prayer and worship as a family to you? Resolve to find books and pamphlets on family prayer to help deepen this experience.

- Spend some time thanking God for those people in your life who love you.

**Thursday:** *Ps 95: 1-2, 6-9*
   *Mt 16: 13-23 (Jesus, Peter and the church)*

Of the four evangelists, Matthew alone speaks of Jesus founding a church. He also speaks of the privileged place of Peter as leader of the church — a responsibility so important that Peter's words would become binding for the salvation of souls. But when Peter tried to sway Jesus from his destiny, Jesus rebuked him; as leader of the church, he must learn to submit his will to God's.

- Spend some time with the passage, "Who do you say that I am?" Respond as sincerely as you can.

- How do you feel about the manner in which church authorities exercise power? On what issues do you respect their leadership most? Least?

- Pray that our church leaders may exercise authority wisely.

**Friday:** *Ps 77: 12-16, 21*
   *Mt 16: 24-28 (The meaning of self-denial)*

The gospel says we must die to ourselves, so it is important that we understand what this means. Jesus does not call us to despise ourselves, nor to deny our personal dreams and ambitions — not unless they lead to sin, that is. The self we are to deny is that very strong tendency in all of us to be selfish and unrelated to others — to be ruled over by instinct and desire rather than truth and love. The cross is the way to grow into the higher, spiritual self.

- Look over your past day, focusing on a few key events. What decisions did you make? What were your motives behind these decisions?

- "Incarnation happens with every decision to love," is a doctrine of the mystics. How do you understand this? Pray for the grace to be more conscious of the loving alternatives you have for each decision you make.

**Saturday:** *Ps 18: 2-4, 47, 51*
      *Mt 17: 14-20 (Jesus cures a young boy)*

Jesus' actions among us reveal a God who views suffering and illness as a tragedy. Far from sending misery into our lives, God wants to help us cope with our problems and to struggle through in persistent love. The key to such persistence is faith, however, which we constantly need to pray for.

- How do you feel about the impatience shown by Jesus in today's reading? Does this make it easier for you to believe in him?

- Think of several ways you could complete this open-ended sentence: "If I had more faith, I could . . ." Examine your responses and ask God to grant you the faith you need to accomplish one of these dreams in the near future.

# Nineteenth Week in Ordinary Time

**Monday:** *Ps 147: 12-15, 19-20*
     *Mt 17: 22-27 (The Temple tax)*

Although Jesus was very careful to avoid proclaiming himself as the Son of God, today's reading alludes to this claim. Since the Temple was considered God's house, he explained, he, son of the king of creation, should not have to pay the Temple tax. Matthew alone carries this story and the account of Peter extracting the coin from a fish (perhaps an allusion to Peter's trade).

- How do you feel about cheating on income taxes?

- "God helps those who help themselves," is a popular saying. Do you believe this? Why? (Why not?)

**Tuesday:** *Dt 32: 3-4, 7-0, 12*
     *Mt 18: 1-5, 10, 12-14 (Childlike faith)*

Acknowledging the fact of our absolute dependence on grace is the first step toward spiritual growth. People who are self-important cut themselves off from grace. That is why Jesus holds out a little child as a model for us, assuring us that our standards of importance are not God's.

- In what ways are you aware of being dependent on God? Do you believe that you have accomplished anything without God's help?

• The parable of the lost sheep teaches us that God loves individuals and not just collectives. Spend some time simply relaxing in the awareness that God loves you, knows you, and delights in you.

**Wednesday:** *Ps 66: 1-3, 5, 8, 16-17*
           *Mt 18: 15-20 (Reconciliation process)*

Because the kingdom of God is characterized by people living in deep, growing relationships, we must make every effort to be reconciled with one another when our differences separate us. If our individual efforts fail, then we should seek help. There may come a point beyond which we will find reconciliation impossible, but we should not be too hasty in drawing this conclusion.

• Which do you find easier: to attempt reconciliation with those you are separated from, or to remain angry and justified against them? How does each response affect your attitude toward others?

• How do you feel about praying with other people? What do verses 19-20 promise?

**Thursday:** *Ps 114: 1-6*
          *Mt 18: 21-19: 1 (The mercy of God)*

Forgiveness is one of the most humbling of all practices; it is also one of the most difficult. That is why Peter asked Jesus if there was a limit to the number of times that forgiveness could be extended by us and by God. Jesus' reply revealed the incomprehensible depths of God's forgiveness, and the awesome responsibility that is ours to extend this grace to others.

• Suppose God were to treat you as you have treated other people: How well would you fare? Which would you prefer to have God extend to you: justice or mercy?

• Is it difficult for you to forgive those who have wronged you? Is it difficult to ask for forgiveness when you've done wrong to another?

• Pray for the grace to know that you are a forgiven sinner.

**Friday:** *Ps 136: 1-3, 16-18, 21-22, 24*
        *Mt 19: 3-12 (Marriage and divorce)*

To understand the significance of today's reading, we must first realize that some Jewish traditions permitted a man to divorce his wife if he simply lost interest in her or found her wanting in household skills. Jesus counters this tradition by holding out as God's will the indissolubility of the marriage commitment. He also states that some people would be better off not married.

• Several of the early Fathers of the church believed that God frowned on sexual intercourse, and that the Holy Spirit deserted people during sex. What would you respond to such an assertion?

- Why would an adult person *choose* to remain unmarried? Do you believe this is healthy?

**Saturday:** *Ps 16: 1-2, 5, 7-8, 11*
     *Mt 19: 13-15 (Jesus and the children)*

Jesus' kindness was shared with all, especially the little and unimportant people in society. He saw the innocence and potential in children and loved them without reserve. Today's reading describes one of the most touching of all encounters between Jesus and people in the Bible.

- George Macdonald used to say that children should not be afraid of the follower of Jesus. Do you agree? How do you feel about children?

- How do you feel about abortion? Have you taken a stand to help people who are struggling with this issue?

# Twentieth Week in Ordinary Time

**Monday:** *Ps 106: 34-40, 43-44*
*Mt 19: 16-22 (The rich young man)*

This is a parable for today's people. Jesus told the rich young man that it was not enough that he was keeping the Law, but challenged him to throw away false securities and become a disciple. Unfortunately, the young man found this invitation too difficult to accept.

- The philosopher Schopenhauer stated that life vacillates between suffering (the fate of the poor and broken) and boredom (the fate of the rich and secure). Do you agree?

- St. Paul stated that the love of money is the root of all evil. How much money do you need to support the lifestyle you believe Christ is calling you to?

- Pray for the grace to be more attached to the things of God.

**Tuesday:** *Ps 85: 9, 11-14*
*Mt 10: 23-30 (Wealth and salvation)*

Monetary wealth is attractive because it affords us numerous opportunities for entertainment, education and influence unavailable to the poor. Money is therefore a primary competitor with God for the hearts of people. In today's reading, Jesus promises a wealth of experience to those who decide to embrace his way.

- "The state of life is most happy where superfluities are not required and necessities are not wanting," wrote Plutarch. What are some of the superfluities of time commitments and possessions that clutter your life? How willing are you to part with these?

- Make a list of possessions you believe to be necessary and important for anyone seeking to grow in Christ.

**Wednesday:** *Ps 21: 2-7*
   *Mt 20: 1-16 (The first and the last)*

At first glance, there seems to be an injustice glossed over by Jesus in today's reading. Although each group got what it had agreed upon, it does seem that the partiality shown the last workers is a slight against the long-suffering group. This is a parable about the kingdom of God, however, pointing out that being with God will be reward aplenty for anyone, no matter how much the person may "deserve" admittance.

- Do you believe that it is "fair" that the good thief on the cross was promised salvation by Jesus when so many of us have to work our whole lives through in faithfulness?

- "A person is not a Christian if his first concern is pay," wrote William Barclay. What should be the first concern of a Christian when considering employment?

**Thursday:** *Ps 40: 5, 7-10*
  *Mt 22: 1-14 (The great banquet)*

Today's parable gives us another important insight into the heart of God, teaching us that God is extremely eager to share his blessings with us. If we are to gain access to these blessings, we must put on the garment of faith, without which we shall never appreciate the things of God.

- What are some of the blessings you have received from the church during the past month (meaning, here, church as people of God)? Thank God for these blessings.

- Ignatian spirituality has it that joy springs from gratitude, which springs from awareness of grace, which springs from faith. Are you a joyful person? What does this say about the way you recognize grace?

**Friday:** *Ps 146: 5-10*
  *Mt 22: 34-40 (The two great
    commandments)*

Still trying to discredit Jesus, the Pharisees attempt to bait him into heresy. Jesus again proves the wiser, simplifying the Old Testament to two laws of love, both of which are dependent and inseparable.

- "The brotherhood of man is impossible unless we recognize the fatherhood of God," wrote Taylor Caldwell. Do you agree?

- "You are as close to God as you are to your

neighbor," goes another popular saying. Think
of one way to show love to the five most important people in your life during the next week.

**Saturday:** *Ps 128: 1-5*
   *Mt 23: 1-12 (Humility and truth)*

"Do as they say, but not as they do," Jesus
counseled his disciples regarding their relationship with the scribes and Pharisees. The apparent
dichotomy in this advice was necessary because
Jesus respected the authority of Jewish religious
leaders while disagreeing with their behavior.
The principles they taught were valid, but pride
discredited their being models.

• Many theologians believe that humility means
  being truthful about our weaknesses *and* our
  strengths. How does this differ from the more
  traditional understanding of humility?

• How do you feel toward proud people? Is there
  anything you can do to become truly humble?
  Apply your suggestions toward your own pride
  as well.

• Pray for the grace to grow in humility.

# Twenty-first Week in Ordinary Time

**Monday:** *Ps 149: 1-6, 9*
   *Mt 23: 13-22 (Jesus confronts the Jewish authorities)*

It is the goal of love to nurture people toward growth. But what if people are "stuck" in stagnation because of wrong-headed thinking or self-righteousness? In today's reading, we note Jesus confronting several erroneous practices of the scribes and Pharisees, hoping to thus call them out of their hypocrisy.

- Do you find it hard to confront a friend or relative who is doing wrong? How about a person who just seems to be stuck in a rut: Can you ask that person how he or she is doing without being nosey?

- How would you respond to a person who says, "Christians should mind their own business unless something or someone affects them personally?"

- Pray for the grace to care enough for others to challenge them to grow.

**Tuesday:** *Ps 139: 1-3, 4-6*
   *Mt 23: 23-26 (Keeping priorities straight)*

Every Jew acknowledged the importance of paying tithes on crops grown. The fact that the

scribes and Pharisees extended this responsibility
to small plots of kitchen seasonings indicated to
Jesus just how off-center they had gotten in their
legalistic zeal. He goes on to say that commitments and responsibilities which detract from
justice, mercy and good faith will leave us empty
inside.

- In what does true religion consist? Do any of
  your present commitments and responsibilities
  detract from your practice of true religion?

- What has the cup of your soul been filled with
  lately? Pray for the grace to be filled with love.

**Wednesday:** *Ps 139: 7-12*
    *Mt 23: 27-32 (Jesus denounces hypocrisy)*
    It is unlikely that anyone has ever confronted a
group of people with more fire and sting than
Jesus did the scribes and Pharisees of his day. For
a Jew to come into contact with a tomb was to
become unclean and, hence, unable to share in
the Passover feast. By calling the scribes and
Pharisees whitewashed tombs, Jesus is saying that
their hypocrisy made them and those they con-
tacted spiritually unclean.

- How do you feel about the manner in which
  Jesus confronted the Jewish authorities? Are his
  actions in keeping with a God of love?

- Write out a set of guidelines for confronting
  other people in love. Make a resolution to prac-

tice these principles with someone you are concerned about during the next day.

**Thursday:** *Ps 90: 3-4, 12-14, 17*
*Mt 24: 42-51 (Faithful servants)*

We now begin reflecting on Jesus' promise to
return again. "Stay awake," he counsels us, for
we do not know when he will come nor when we
will die. But the best reason for being faithful is
not fear of punishment; we are to do so because
faithfulness is part of our wholeness.

- During the course of a ball game, one of the
  saints was asked what he would do if he knew
  that the Lord would return to earth in 15
  minutes. "I'd finish this game of ball," he
  replied. Does this describe your attitude?

- "One of the most tragic things I know about
  human nature is that all of us tend to put off
  living," wrote Dale Carnegie. Vow to make the
  most of this day.

**Friday:** *Ps 97: 1-2, 5-6, 10-12*
*Mt 25: 1-13 (Preparedness pays)*

Today's parable is based upon traditions that
seem strange to many of us in the West. After a
couple married, they went to their home and
were given royal treatment by friends and
relatives for several days. Late-comers were
barred from this ceremony. Because no one was
allowed outside at night without a light of some

kind, people waiting for a nocturnal return of the
couple to their home needed plenty of oil if they
were to gain admittance to the ceremony. In the
same way, Jesus tells us, we are to be vigilant for
his return.

- How do you feel when you reflect upon the fact
  that you will die?

- "Those who weep loudest at funerals are those
  who never said, 'I love you,' when they had the
  chance," said Leo Buscaglia. How can you tell
  the people you care for that you love them today?

**Saturday:** *Ps 98: 1, 7-9*
       *Mt 25: 14-30 (Parable of the talents)*
   Today's parable is a powerful expression of
God's hopes and dreams for us. We have each
been given a certain amount of potential, and we
shall be judged according to what we did with
what we have been given. Failure to develop
human potential may well be the gravest of all
sins, for it is a slap in the face to our creator God.

- What do you believe to be your most
  characteristic gifts? How are you using these to
  help build God's kingdom?

- How committed are you to your own personal
  growth? How do you feel when you are not
  growing as a person? How do you feel when
  you are experiencing a period of growth?

- Pray for the grace to love yourself enough to
  want to grow.

# Twenty-second Week
# in Ordinary Time

**Monday:** *Ps 96: 1, 3-5, 11-13*
*Lk 4: 16-30 (Jesus and the Nazarenes)*

From now until Advent, we will be spending time with Luke's gospel. We begin by noting that Jesus was received with mixed reactions by his home folks. At first they were proud of him and of his eloquence, but Jesus was not content to let them bask in the rays of this most shallow of all sources of self-worth. Worth by association counts for nothing if it is not complemented by faith and good works.

- How much self-worth do you derive from supporting certain athletic teams? From belonging to certain civic organizations? From your cultural heritage? From your denomination?

- What source of self-worth does Jesus call us to embrace? Ask for this grace.

**Tuesday:** *Ps 27: 1, 4, 13-14*
*Lk 4: 31-37 (Jesus cures a demoniac)*

Outside his hometown Jesus found people more open to his message and his healing. In today's reading, we learn that he taught with authority, which was quite a novelty compared to the carefully measured words of the Jewish authorities. The Holy Spirit, Jesus' power and souce of authority, silenced other spirits of fragmentation, leaving the people amazed.

- Picture the scene described in today's reading from the standpoint of a member of the crowd. Note Jesus' encounter with the demoniac; hear the demon object to Jesus; see Jesus' face as he touches the man. Listen to the people as they say, "What is there about him?" Let your spirit be buoyed up by his Spirit.

- Pray for the grace to be more self-confident.


**Wednesday:** *Ps 52: 10-11*
      *Lk 4: 38-44 (Jesus' popularity grows)*

No matter where he went, Jesus was followed by large crowds. Many went because they sought healing, but many probably went just out of curiosity. It was because he feared being misunderstood that Jesus forbade the evil spirits to speak of him as the Messiah. He wanted to reach the people without having to work through their preconceptions.

- How does the work you do contribute to the building of God's kingdom? Do you have a sense that your work is what you were "sent" to do? What can you do to make your daily work more enriching to yourself and others?

- Pray for the grace to find ways to love during work time.


**Thursday:** *Ps 98: 2-6*
      *Lk 5: 1-11 (The apostles called)*

We often believe that our successes are due entirely to our own efforts, hence we cultivate a self-righteous attitude that we are deserving of God's favor. In today's reading, Jesus teaches four professional fishermen that without God's grace, they could not catch so much as one single fish. The fishermen respond by following their Lord.

- "Work as if everything depended on you, and pray as if everything depended on God," advised Ignatius of Loyola. How close is this to your own attitude concerning work and grace?

- Spend some time with the passage, "Do not be afraid. From now on you will be catching people." Allow God's desire to minister through you pervade your entire being.

Friday: *Ps 100: 1-5*
    *Lk 5: 33-39 (Jesus, the bridegroom)*

Far from being rigid ascetics, Jesus and his disciples were considered quite "loose" in comparison to several lines of Jewish spirituality. Jesus explained that he and his disciples were more interested in celebrating life than in shriveling up in old traditions.

- What are some of your "old skins" that you find hardest to shed for the sake of the gospel? Pray for the grace to be willing to change these habits.

- Think of something worth celebrating today. Call it to mind several times through the day and share your joy with others.

**Saturday:** *Ps 54: 3-4, 6, 8*
   *Lk 6: 1-5 (Jesus, Lord of the Sabbath)*

Jewish laws were initially established to help Jewish communities live out their covenant with God in solidarity and in order. After a while, however, these laws became idols of sorts, and the focus was no longer on God. Today's gospel describes Jesus confronting one of these many examples of dehumanizing legalism.

• "God's will is the well-being of humanity," wrote Hans Kung. Do you agree with this? Why? (Why not?)

• In your community worship experience, what do you focus on? Is your worship Christ-oriented?

# Twenty-third Week
# in Ordinary Time

**Monday:** *Ps 62: 6-7, 9*
*Lk 6: 6-11 (Healing on the sabbath)*

At times Jesus was intentionally provocative, contrary to popular notions of him as being diplomatic and mild. In today's reading, Luke describes a most significant encounter between Jesus and the Jewish authorities. By healing the man with the withered hand, Jesus was not responding to an emergency allowed on the sabbath; he was proving a point.

• Why do you believe Jesus chose to provoke the authorities? What did he hope to gain by doing so? What did he stand to lose?

• Have you ever found it necessary to be prophetically provocative? Are there at present issues requiring such a stance from you? How will you respond?

• Pray for the grace to be courageous for Christ.

**Tuesday:** *Ps 115: 1-2, 8-11*
*Lk 6: 12-19 (Jesus chooses the Twelve)*

Jesus knew that he would one day die, and he knew that he would not even begin to scratch the surface of a populated earth without the ongoing ministry of his followers through the ages. That is why he called the Twelve to be his followers; that is why he still calls us to minister.

- If someone were to ask you who you are and what is important in this world, how would you answer?

- Spend some time being present to God's healing Spirit.

**Wednesday:** *Ps 145: 2-3, 10-13*
     *Lk 6: 20-26 (Blest are the poor)*

Luke has simplified the list of beatitudes described in Matthew, eliminating material that his non-Jewish audience would not have properly appreciated. Still, we are left with blessings and curses which should deeply challenge our lives.

- Which of the beatitudes do you find most consoling? Why?

- Which of the "woes" disturb you most? Why? How does this challenge you to change?

- Pray for the grace to be willing to change for the sake of the kingdom.

**Thursday:** *Ps 150: 1-6*
     *Lk 6: 27-38 (Love your enemies)*

Jesus never denied that we would have enemies, but he did command us to recognize in our enemies fellow children of God. How to love those with whom we disagree and who oppress people is one of the most challenging tasks facing Christians today. If we do not meet this challenge, we shall be no different than animals, who respond kindly to those who treat them well.

- Do you believe that Christians should do something to resist evils taking place in the world? Do you believe that such resistance ought never to be violent? Why (Why not?)

- How do you feel when your efforts at kindness are not appreciated by others? Why should you persist in kindness? What will happen to *you* if you do not persist?

- Pray for the strength and wisdom to learn to resist evil in love.

**Friday:** *Ps 16: 1-2, 5, 7-8, 11*
*Lk 6: 39-42 (Do not judge)*

Luke's sermon on the plain is similar to Matthew's Sermon on the Mount in that it includes a collection of sayings and teachings of Jesus. Today's reading warns us against limiting our relationships with others by judging them harshly.

- What is the difference between forming an impression or opinion about a person and judging him or her?

- What kinds of judgments are explicit and implicit in racism, sexism and agism? Are you free from these shackles?

• Pray for the grace to be more open to the gifts
  that other people are.


**Saturday:** *Ps 113: 1-7*
       *Lk 6: 43-49 (A firm foundation)*

Human beings were created in such a fashion
that we cannot live our lives immorally and
aspiritually without burning out. "Among all my
patients in the second half of life — that is to say,
over 35 — there has not been one whose problem
in the last resort was not that of finding a
religious outlook on life," wrote Carl Jung. Today's reading expresses the importance of this
religious foundation.

• "The figure of Christ seems to be the only one
  toward which human nature can tend without
  becoming wearied or deformed," wrote
  Teilhard de Chardin. Do you agree?

• What does Jesus Christ mean to you?

# Twenty-fourth Week
# in Ordinary Time

**Monday:** *Ps 28: 2, 7-9*
*Lk 7: 1-10 (Jesus heals a gentile's servant)*

"With God, all things are possible," we say at one time or another. But do we believe this? Those who do might discover, like the centurion in today's reading, that God cannot resist helping us when we are truly submissive to his will in faith and hope.

- During what period of your life was your faith strongest? How would you describe the strength of your faith at present?

- Why did the Jews plead on behalf of the centurion? What does this say about the power of love?

- Pray for the grace to grow more deeply in faith.

**Tuesday:** *Ps 101: 1-3, 5-6*
*Lk 7: 11-17 (Jesus raises a boy in Naim)*

Jesus' actions in today's readings show us that God views the death of young people to be a tragedy. In vain do we search for mysterious and hidden designs to help us understand how God could permit such tragedies, for it is his will that we eventually eliminate them. The suffering of a woman whose child has died shall forever move the heart of Jesus.

- Do you believe in bad and good luck? Do you believe that everything that happens to people is God's will?

- Picture this scene in your imagination from the standpoint of a disciple. Hear the wailing of the mourners as you approach the town; note the agony on the face of the mother; watch Jesus as he intervenes; experience the wonder of the moment as the boy returns to life.

**Wednesday:** *Ps 111: 1-6*
    *Lk 7: 31-35 (You can't please everyone)*

There were those who thought that John the Baptist was fanatical in his asceticism; most likely, these same people believed that Jesus was excessive in his sensual enjoyments. Jesus was undaunted by these kinds of criticisms, however, for he did not come to please the crowds, but to do his Father's will.

- Do you enjoy sensual pleasures when experienced appropriately? Do you seek out opportunities to experience sensual pleasures like good food, fresh air, sunsets, and hugs and kisses?

- Pray for openness to the graces that come to us through creation.

**Thursday:** *Ps 111: 7-10*
    *Lk 7: 36-50 (Jesus, the Pharisees, and the prostitute)*

In order to appreciate the meaning of today's reading, we need to realize that Simon the Pharisee had denied Jesus several hospitable gestures normally extended to guests in a Jewish home. When a woman reputed to be a sinner extended these to Jesus, he pointed out the relationship between her generosity and her acceptance of forgiveness.

- For what do you need to ask God's forgiveness right now? Spend some time allowing God's forgiving grace to deepen your own self-acceptance.

- Have you taken your loved ones for granted lately? If so, ask for their forgiveness and vow to start again.

- Pray for the grace to experience God's forgiveness.

**Friday:** *Ps 49: 0-10, 17-20*
     *Lk 8: 1-3 (Jesus and the women)*

"It is one of the supreme achievements of Jesus that he can enable the most diverse people to live together without in the least losing their own personalities or qualities," wrote William Barclay. And the group of women who followed Jesus was indeed a diverse band! Common to all of them, however, was their love for Jesus and their commitment to serve him out of their own meager resources.

- Do you find it difficult to establish friendships with people of opposite views? Why? (Why not?)

- Do you believe that community is richer for including a diversity of people? Does your community include that diversity?


**Saturday:** *Ps 100: 2-5*
  *Lk 8: 4-15 (The parable of the good seed)*

Many scholars believe that the parables of Jesus are probably the best-preserved, least-manipulated accounts of his teachings. That is because stories are more easily remembered and seem to suffer less change through oral tradition than do other kinds of teachings. Today's reading gives us a glimpse of Jesus' vision of his work. He saw himself as a seed sower, and realized that not everyone would appreciate his words, but felt that those who did so made it all worthwhile.

- What does success mean to you? Are you able to accept yourself if you do not achieve 100 percent of what you set out to do?

- What kind of seed have you been sowing in your home lately? In your Christian community? At work?

- Spend some time inviting the Spirit to cultivate good soil in your heart.

# Twenty-fifth Week in Ordinary Time

**Monday:** *Ps 126: 1-6*
 *Lk 8: 16-18 (Parable of the lamp)*

God has blessed us with innumerable graces, bringing light to our lives. With grace comes the responsibility to extend grace to others. When we do so, we discover that special dynamism of life alluded to by James in today's reading: Those who risk and engage themselves in life will grow in grace and experience; those who do nothing will regress.

- Make a list of the ten people to whom you are closest. How does each person enrich your life? What would your life be like without these people? Thank God for the graces they bring to you.

- "If you don't use it, you lose it," goes an old biological dictum. Have you been remiss in investing any of your gifts in the service of the kingdom lately? Are you willing to let yourself regress in this area?

**Tuesday:** *Ps 122: 1-5*
 *Lk 8: 19-21 (The Lord's family)*

It is typical of Luke that he has taken the sting out of some of the more unsettling accounts about Jesus found in Mark and Matthew. Mark wrote that Jesus' family was concerned for his sanity, but Luke simply has them paying a visit to Jesus. At any rate, Jesus uses the occasion to affirm the primacy of our brotherhood and sisterhood under God.

- What is the meaning for you of communion of saints, i.e., that those who have died in Christ continue to work with us and intercede for us as we struggle to do God's will?

- Who is your favorite saint? How did this person reveal God? Thank God that such a person has blessed your life.

**Wednesday:** *Tb 13: 2-8*
       *Lk 9: 1-6 (The twelve emissaries)*

In order that the twelve apostles not be judged as having hidden agenda and ulterior motives, Jesus sent them out among the people as poor, unassuming messengers. They were to extend God's gifts of healing and teaching in return for food and shelter. If rejected, they were to move along. It is a model of ministry profound in its simplicity.

- Make a list of ulterior motives that seem to hamper the efforts of Christian ministers. Do any of these motives interfere with your own efforts at spreading the Good News?

- What does the virtue of simplicity mean to you?

**Thursday:** *Ps 149: 1-6, 9*
       *Lk 9: 7-9 (Herod's paranoia)*

If modern psychology has taught us anything, it is that we cannot escape the problems of life by burying our feelings. Herod the Great is a case in point. Guilt-ridden because of his execution of John the Baptist, he began to believe that John had risen in the person of Jesus.

- Are there crises and tragedies in your past that you have not yet finished dealing with? If so, are you willing to seek out help to work your way through them?

- When was the last time you got angry at someone? How did you resolve the conflict? What did you do with your feelings of anger? (If you did nothing with them, know that conflicts with this person will most likely return.)

**Friday:** *Ps 43: 1-4*
       *Lk 9: 18-22 (Jesus and prayer)*

It is characteristic of Luke to portray Jesus as a man of prayer. Before undertaking major endeavors, Jesus is shown spending time in prayer, a modeling which we can scarcely afford to ignore. In today's reading, prayer precedes Jesus' disclosure to his apostles of himself as a suffering redeemer.

- Why do you pray? How has prayer helped you lately?

- Why do you believe Jesus had to "endure many sufferings, be rejected by the elders, the high priests and the scribes, and be put to death"?

- Pray for the grace to be more centered in the Spirit of Jesus.

**Saturday:** *Jer 31: 10-13*
  *Lk 9: 43-45 (Passion predictions)*

During the height of Jesus' ministry — when everything seemed to be moving along almost unbelievably well — he often warned his apostles that the tide would one day turn and he would have to suffer and die. Later, they would appreciate his efforts to prepare them, but at the time, it was a message that confused them.

- Do you believe that God wanted Jesus to be crucified?

- "Jesus died for me," we often hear Christians saying. What does this statement mean to you?

- Spend some time thanking God for the gift of his Son.

# Twenty-sixth Week in Ordinary Time

**Monday:** *Ps 102: 16-23, 29*
    *Lk 9: 46-50 (Who is the greatest?)*

As Jesus' reputation spread throughout the countryside, it was only natural that the disciples should vie for status. Christian identity has nothing to do with status or a competitive edge, however. True greatness is bestowed upon people who are open to accepting grace as a little child.

• How important is status and recognition to you? With whom do you compare yourself in evaluating your worth as a person?

• Pray for the grace to form your identity more deeply in Christ.

**Tuesday:** *Ps 87: 1-7*
    *Lk 9: 51-56 (The journey to Jerusalem)*

Chapters 9-18 in Luke differ from Mark and Matthew in that Jesus is shown journeying to Jerusalem, where he anticipates his decisive confrontation with the authorities. This literary organization is designed to help us appreciate the meaning of Jesus' life and ministry. In today's reading, he proceeds through hostile territory, reprimanding James and John for their impulsive vindictiveness.

- Jesus could probably have escaped to foreign
  lands and lived to a ripe old age as a venerated
  teacher and healer. Why do you believe he
  chose instead to journey to Jerusalem, where
  conflict was certain?

- "Don't rock the boat," goes a rule implicit in
  bureaucracies of all kinds. How much of this
  spirit has pervaded your outlook? When is it
  appropriate to "rock the boat"? What are the
  risks?

**Wednesday:** *Ps 137: 1-6*
        *Lk 9: 57-62 (A time for decision)*
Following Jesus means placing his principles
before all others and immediately aligning our
lives with his. In today's reading, we see that
hesitation and excessive prudence can sometimes
prevent us from making a full response to Jesus.

- Some have said that prudence should not be
  considered a Christian virtue. Do you agree?

- Do you believe that you are living out a full
  response to Jesus' invitation to follow him?

- Spend some time with the passage, "Now is the
  time of salvation."

**Thursday:** *Ps 19: 8-11*
        *Lk 10: 1-12 (The 72 emissaries)*
Lacking the advantages of modern media to

publicize his visitations, Jesus designated 72 disciples to prepare the way before him. Most noteworthy is the statement that he sent them out in pairs. Married couples might well claim this passage as an affirmation of their own discipleship; single people and celibates must recognize in it a statement pointing out the need for ministerial support.

- "If there is a person in your life who knows you and accepts you with all your faults, you will probably never have to worry about your mental health," said Carl Jung. Do you have such a person in your life? If not, resolve to find a spiritual director who can offer you such a grace.

- "People are lonely because they build walls instead of bridges," wrote Joseph Newton. Do you agree? Looking over your day to come, anticipate times when you can build bridges.

**Friday:** *Ps 79: 1-5, 8-9*
         *Lk 10: 13-16 (Townships cursed)*

Today we again return to the sobering theme of procrastinating in our response to Christ. Jesus cursed Chorazin, Bethsaida and Capernaum because they did not respond when the offer of salvation was opened to them. We, too, should not take for granted Jesus' invitation to follow

him. Furthermore, there are times in our lives
when we are especially aware of this offer, and
our responses then are most important to our for-
mation.

• "It only takes a moment to be loved a whole life
  through," said John Powell. Have you experienced such peak moments in your life? Did
  you ever withdraw from the promise of such a
  moment? Pray for the grace to recognize and
  accept these invitations when they come.

• Spend some time with the verse, "He who hears
  you, hears me." What does this say to you
  about the importance of your example before
  others?

**Saturday:** *Ps 69: 33-37*
     *Lk 10: 17-24 (The joy of Jesus)*

Is there more to life than pleasurable experiences or happiness? Yes, there is the joy of the
Holy Spirit, as today's reading shows us. While
pleasure comes with sensual gratification and is
short-lived, and happiness comes from striving to
realize personal goals, joy is deeper, being rooted
in an awareness of the great things God has done
for us.

• What kind of person do you believe you would
  be if you were not a Christian? Spend some
  time considering the many ways your Christian
  faith has helped to make you a better person.

- Pray with Jesus, "I offer you grateful praise, O
  Father, Lord of heaven and earth." Repeat this
  prayer of praise again and again as your heart
  wells up with joy.

# Twenty-seventh Week in Ordinary Time

**Monday:** *Jon 2: 2-5, 8*
*Lk 10: 25-37 (Parable of the Good Samaritan)*

"And who is my neighbor?" the lawyer asked Jesus in earnest. Many rabbis interpreted God's commandment to love the neighbor as a summons to love only Jews. Jesus countered this elitism by posing a story about a Samaritan who was a model of the true neighbor, closer to God's heart than the Jewish priest who hurried along and ignored the man on the side of the road. Since Samaritans were despised by the Jews, Jesus' parable must have stung his listeners.

- Who are the "people in the bushes" ignored in today's world? How do you respond to their needs?

- "Jesus was the only teacher tall enough to see over the fences that divide the human race into compartments," wrote Frank Crane. Pray for the grace to be able to see people as Christ sees them.

**Tuesday:** *Ps 130: 1-4, 7-8*
*Lk 10: 38-42 (Mary and Martha)*

In life we constantly have to make decisions, for at any moment there are a number of items to which we can direct our attention. In the story of

Mary and Martha, Jesus affirms Mary because she has chosen wisely in setting her priorities. The dishes could be done at any time, and Martha's fretting over the "details of hospitality" were not so important as being present to the Son of God.

• How do you make value decisions concerning the focus of your attention through each day? What happens to your attention when you do not consciously direct it toward some external or internal matter?

• "God does not want our presents; he wants our presence," according to an old aphorism. Spend some time simply being present to the Lord, basking in the rays of his love.

**Wednesday:** *Ps 86: 3-6, 9-10*
*Lk 11: 1-4 (The Lord's Prayer)*

Luke's version of the prayer of Jesus is shorter than Matthew's and is characteristic of his commitment to simplify the words of Jesus. We are nonetheless left with the essentials emphasized in Matthew's version: praise, kingdom, dependence, forgiveness and perseverance.

• Which phrase from the Lord's Prayer do you find easiest to pray? Which is most difficult? Why?

• What kind of God does Jesus reveal through this prayer?

**Thursday:** *Ps 1: 1-6*
   *Lk 11: 5-13 (The value of persistence)*

Jesus often taught about God by using analogies from human behavior. One of his most frequent themes is that God is at least as good as are good human beings. God is therefore approachable, interested and willing to help us if we but take the trouble to address him.

- "The poor man is not he who is without a cent, but he who is without a dream," wrote Harry Kemp. What are some of your dreams for the future? How do you keep these dreams alive?

- What are you doing to keep yourself growing and learning about the spiritual life?

- Pray for the grace to dream "the impossible dream."

**Friday:** *Ps 9: 2-3, 6, 16*
   *Lk 11: 15-26 (Jesus and Beelzebul)*

In order to discredit Jesus' ministry, certain people began accusing him of doing the work of Satan. Jesus not only counters the contradictions apparent in such accusations, but also states that people who are not with him are working against him. There is really no middle ground in life upon which a person may stand in neutrality toward God.

- Looking back over the events of the past several days, do you see yourself moving toward or away from God? Explain.

- What kind of "unclean spirit" has been troubling you lately? How can you displace it with love? Make a plan, and pray for the grace to carry out your resolve.

**Saturday:** *Ps 97: 1-2, 5-6, 11-12*
       *Lk 11: 27-28 (True blessings)*

Again we hear a message ringing through the gospels: Knowing Jesus and simply being related to him in a superficial way counts for nothing. "Even the devils believe in God," St. James wrote, and they recognized Jesus to be the Messiah. If we are to really grow in Christ, we must act on God's word.

- Which Christian values do you have the most trouble understanding? Resolve to speak to someone who can help you to comprehend what God is calling you to in this area.

- Spend some time with the verse, "Blest are (you) when you hear the word of God and keep it."

# Twenty-eighth Week in Ordinary Time

**Monday:** *Ps 98: 1-4*
 *Lk 11: 29-32 (Seekers of grace)*

There are people living in countries where the freedom to worship is diminished or prohibited by oppressive governments. The least that those of us who live in free countries can do is to take advantage of the many opportunities for growth present in our society. Jesus commended the Queen of Sheba and the Ninevites for making the most of their opportunities to grow in grace; he affirms us if we do likewise.

- When was the last time you made a retreat or day of recollection? Look into the possibility of scheduling one soon.

- What are some signs of God's presence that you have noted recently? Thank God for these reassurances of his love for you.

**Tuesday:** *Ps 19: 2-5*
 *Lk 11: 37-41 (Confrontation at a Pharisee's home)*

Some of the Pharisees must have been friendly toward Jesus' cause. Indeed, St. Paul often found them to be more sympathetic to the gospel than were the scribes or the Sadducees. When Jesus chose to ignore certain rituals of cleanliness in a Pharisee's home, he was being deliberately provocative. This incident gave him an opportunity to confront the legalism of his host and, hence, call him to re-examine his priorities.

- Many people believe that Jesus' criticism of the Pharisee in today's reading might well be applied to society today. What do you think?

- Why would alms-giving help to transform the heart of the Pharisees? How does giving of your time and talent in the service of others transform you?

**Wednesday:** *Ps 62: 2-3, 6-7, 9*
       *Lk 11: 42-46 ("Woe to you . . .")*

If we saw a friend backing toward the edge of a cliff, we would certainly yell out a warning. Similarly, Jesus felt that love compelled him to warn the scribes and Pharisees that some of their beliefs and practices were hurting them and others as well.

- "He has the right to criticize who has the heart to help," wrote Abraham Lincoln. Does this criterion apply to Jesus?

- Of what practices in the church are you most critical? What are you doing to help to better this situation?

**Thursday:** *Ps 130: 1-6*
       *Lk 11: 47-54 (More woes)*

How easy it is to honor a holy person after

they've died, but how difficult to tolerate the words and deeds of a living saint. When Jesus confronted the scribes and Pharisees for precisely this hypocrisy, he aroused only their animosity. They were too proud to change.

- Of what practices in our society are you most critical? What are you doing to help to better this situation?

- Do you avoid arguments when it is obvious that participants are not open to changing? Why? (Why not?)

**Friday:** *Ps 32: 1-2, 5, 11*
        *Lk 12: 1-7 (Fear God alone)*

People who are afraid are not free, Jesus tells us in today's reading. "Perfect love casts out all fear," St. John wrote in his epistle. If we could eliminate from our lives the fear of death and the fear of harsh judgments from others, we would indeed be free. If we really believed that God loved us unconditionally, this fear would leave us.

- When do you most often experience fear and anxiety? How do you usually handle these feelings? How can you reframe these fearful occasions in your thinking to diminish fear? Write out suggestions to yourself.

- Spend some time with the verse, "Fear nothing, then. You are worth more than a flock of sparrows."

**Saturday:** *Ps 105: 6-9, 42-43*
   *Lk 12: 8-12 (The unforgivable sin)*

It takes faith and courage to publicly affirm Jesus as Lord and Savior of our lives and of the world. To deny that God can change a person, however, is to sin against the Holy Spirit, for such a denial makes one incapable of repenting and laying hold on the only source of grace. How terrible for us when we have lost such faith in God!

• Have you ever given up on yourself and your ability to cope with life? If so, spend a few moments reflecting on how far you have come since then.

• How have you acknowledged the Son of Man at work lately? At home? How will you acknowledge him before people today?

• Pray for the grace to be true to your faith in times of crisis.

# Twenty-ninth Week in Ordinary Time

**Monday:** *Ps 100: 2-5*
*Lk 12: 13-21 (On materialism)*

We should never make the mistake of assuming that Christianity is completely unconcerned with material goods. How cruel it would be for a Christian to chide a person who is hungry or unemployed because he or she is not concerned about spiritual matters! Jesus recognized the fact of our human need for basic material goods, but warned us not to look to these transient riches for security.

- Spend some time with the verse, "A person may be wealthy, but possessions will not guarantee life." What, or who can guarantee life?

- Is it possible for a person to be a follower of Jesus and be wealthy? Why? (Why not?)

**Tuesday:** *Ps 40: 7-10, 17*
*Lk 12: 35-38 (Stay awake)*

How wonderful it is to love someone and to be aware that this person is watching your every move in utter delight! This is exactly how God regards us. As we grow in our love of God, we shall become more aware and eager to be completely united with him.

- Many philosophers have said that consciousness is what makes us different from animals. Do you agree?

- Stop many times today to spend a few moments contemplating the wonder of a God who loves you and delights in you. Let this wonder refresh you.

**Wednesday:** *Ps 124: 1-8*
     *Lk 12: 39-48 (Honesty and fidelity)*

The world is a much better place because of the Judeo-Christian doctrine of an eventual call to judgment. But fear of punishment is, at best, only a minimal reason to remain faithful to God. Fidelity to Christ's values is strongest in people who recognize in these principles a way to live life to the full. Those who never achieve this understanding will not be judged as harshly as will those who do know the truth, but choose selfishness anyway.

- What are some of the reasons why you are faithful to following Christ?

- "When you know the right thing to do, but do not do it, you sin," wrote St. James. Spend some time reflecting on how you have lately fallen short of the goodness Christ calls you to. Ask God for forgiveness.

**Thursday:** *Ps 1: 1-6*
      *Lk 12: 49-53 (The fire of Christ)*

"Peace at any price" is no slogan for a Christian to adopt as a guiding principle. Although it is true that Jesus is often called the Prince of Peace, we must realize that the peace he brings cannot exist outside of a context of truth and love. Some people will not recognize truth, others will reject love; therefore, Christians ought to expect persecutions.

• "If you want peace, work for justice," reads a slogan adopted by the U.S. Catholic bishops. Do you agree with this slogan? Why? (Why not?)

• Has your Christian faith brought divisions in your family? If so, what can you do to remain related to family members without compromising your beliefs?

**Friday:** *Ps 119: 66, 68, 76-77, 93-94*
      *Lk 12: 54-59 (The signs of the times)*

We have become quite adept at understanding God's creation and of prospering from it. We have placed people on the moon and learned the secrets of the atom. We have a technology that promises wonders only dreamed of by science-fiction writers in the past. Yet we have achieved only minimal ethical and spiritual progress through the ages. In today's reading, Jesus tells us that we ought to apply our intelligence to the things of God as much as to creation and materialism.

- "People do not change, only culture," goes a maxim often heard. Do you agree with this? Why? (Why not?)

- What are some of the signs of the times today that we ought to pay more attention to? What are you doing to take a stand?

**Saturday:** *Ps 24: 1-6*
   *Lk 13: 1-9 (The patience of Christ)*

In today's reading, Jesus teaches us a lesson that goes against many popular notions. Galileans murdered by Pilate and people killed by a falling tower were simply victims of circumstances, he tells us. Never let us suppose that tragedy is a judgment of God against someone. Let us instead be compassionate toward the unfortunate, for their fate is not necessarily deserved.

- Do you believe that God causes human suffering? What can we learn from suffering if we persevere in faith and love?

- How do you feel toward those less fortunate than yourself? What do you do with your feelings of self-righteousness?

- Pray for the grace to be more accepting of yourself and others.

# Thirtieth Week in Ordinary Time

**Monday:** *Ps 68: 2, 4, 6-7, 20-21*
  *Lk 13: 10-17 (Jesus heals on the sabbath)*

Today's reading teaches us a very important lesson. By healing a woman on the sabbath, Jesus provoked the wrath of the chief of the synagogue. He responded to this indignation by pointing out that people are more important than animals and even laws. Christianity alone is the religion of the individual.

• Do you believe that the Spirit of Jesus heals today? If you do, then how is God working healing through you?

• Have you neglected contacting certain friends and family members lately? Resolve to communicate with at least two with whom you have lost touch during the coming week.


**Tuesday:** *Ps 126: 1-5*
  *Lk 13: 18-21 (Growth of the kingdom)*

Is history going somewhere? This is a very important question, and different religions give different replies. Eastern religions like Buddhism and Hinduism espouse a circular view of history, with little or no real progress being made in human spiritual growth. Religions springing from the Judeo-Christian tradition propose a linear view of history, with progress unto the full realization of God's kingdom growing slowly but surely through the years — as does a mustard seed into a shrub and yeast through a batch of dough.

- Do you believe that individuals can change for the better through the years? Do you believe that societies can change for the better? Why? (Why not?)

- Spend some time being present to God, asking that the Holy Spirit leaven your own spirit unto love.

**Wednesday:** *Ps 13: 4-6*
　　　　*Lk 13: 22-30 (The narrow gate)*

If we have not already heard this message enough, we need to listen again: Salvation does not come because we know about Jesus. In today's reading, we hear Jesus promising to reject people who claim familiarity with him, but who did nothing to help their neighbors in need. The narrow road he invites us to walk is the difficult path of love.

- Do you believe that some people will go to hell, i.e., shall be separated from God for all eternity? Why? (Why not?)

- List some of the key events of your past two days. How would you describe the spiritual road that threads through these events?

- Pray for the grace to embrace difficult times in a spirit of perseverance.

**Thursday:** *Ps 109: 21-22, 26-27, 30-31*
    *Lk 13: 31-35 (Jesus and Herod)*

Herod was king of Galilee, but was little more than a puppet of Rome. Still feeling guilty over his murder of John the Baptist, he decided to kill Jesus, who reminded him of John. But friendly Pharisees tipped Jesus off, alerting him to the danger. Jesus had his heart set on Jerusalem, however, and was not to be denied his destiny.

- What kind of man calls a king a fox? Why was Jesus unafraid of Herod?

- What are some of the key secular issues of the day? How are you taking a stand?

**Friday:** *Ps 147: 12-15, 19-20*
    *Lk 14: 1-6 (Healing again on the sabbath)*

Although Luke does not say it explicitly, one can sense that the reason the Pharisee invited Jesus to his home was so he could keep an eye on him and store up information to use to discredit him. Jesus again decided to challenge the Pharisees to leave their legalism behind and embrace the law of love.

- What are some of the idols of the day which deny the value of the individual? How are you taking a stand to work through these influences?

- Pray for the grace to see people as more important than anything else.

**Saturday:** *Ps 94: 12-18*
*Lk 14: 1, 7-11 (The first and the last)*

Still under close surveillance, Jesus refused to take on a defensive posture toward the Pharisees. Social status was a primary hindrance to spiritual growth for many of them, so he found a teachable moment at a dinner party to invite them to become truly humble.

- Do you know a friend or family member who is following the idol of social status? How can you confront this person in a manner that shows your love and concern for his or her spiritual growth?

- Do you discipline your own desires to impress others for the sake of your ego? Make a plan to stave off this weakness when it occurs.

# Thirty-first Week in Ordinary Time

**Monday:** *Ps 69: 30-31, 33-37*
     *Lk 14: 12-14 (Agape love)*

In order to suggest a discipline that would help the Pharisees work through their preoccupation over status and discover agape, the love which God shows for us, Jesus suggested that they reach out to those who could not possibly repay them. If we, too, were to take him up on this, we would discover an opportunity to love as God loves.

- Have you ever loved or given with no expectation of return? If so, get in touch with the feelings you had when you did so. If not, think of a way to do so today.

- Why do you believe God loves you? Pray for the grace to view other people likewise.

**Tuesday:** *Ps 131: 1-3*
     *Lk 14: 15-24 (Good excuses for the damned)*

God created because God is love, and love seeks to share its joy with others. He chose a people and attempted to prepare them to appreciate the gifts he wanted to share with them — especially his Son — but they were too busy with their own agenda. Therefore, Jesus tells us in today's reading, the invitation shall now be extended to anyone who wants to share in the joy of the Lord.

- "Life is what happens to us while we're making other plans," wrote Ann Landers. What do you think she meant by this?

- What are some of the excuses you use to keep yourself distanced from the needs of others? How many of these are really legitimate?

**Wednesday:** *Ps 112: 1-2, 4-5, 9*
   *Lk 14: 25-33 (Pick up your cross)*

The cross is such a powerful Christian symbol because it describes so well the quality of love which God expects of us. Christianity alone has been able to extract meaning from human suffering, for our God has suffered with us. Those who decide to follow Christ can expect to experience struggles and hardships, but perseverance will bring deeper love and new life.

- What kind of battle plan have you drawn up for your life? What kinds of obstacles can frustrate these plans? Where does the cross figure in?

- Pray for the grace to remain faithful to Christ when inconveniences confront you.

**Thursday:** *Ps 27: 1, 4, 13-14*
   *Lk 15: 1-10 (Two parables of mercy)*

God's will may sometimes be difficult to discern, but we may always be certain that it is his wish that people come to know and love him.

We should therefore pray for those who have fallen away and make every effort to help turn souls toward Christ. When we do so, we can expect to share in the joy of the angels.

- Do you feel that it is any of your business to try to influence other people to embrace faith in Christ? Why? (Why not?)

- If a person is kind and virtuous but does not believe in Jesus, should a Christian try to influence him or her to become a believer?

- Pray that those who reach out in the love of Christ may persevere in love.

**Friday:** *Ps 98: 1-4*
   *Lk 16: 1-8 (The clever manager)*

At first glance, this appears to be a parable of forgiveness, but there is more to it than that. When Jesus commends the manager for his cleverness in assuring his future, he also chides his followers for their lack of initiative for the things of God. What if we really decided to give as much time and effort toward building the kingdom of God as we do to securing a living and advancing ourselves professionally? What kind of world would it be if everyone did so?

- Divide a sheet of paper into three columns. In the first column, list activities that you are engaged in regularly (employment, sleeping, recreation, etc.). In the second column, list the amount of time you spend each week for each activity in column one. In the third column, list the reasons why you engage in each activity. Study this list awhile, praying for wisdom to help you reorganize your life, if necessary.

**Saturday:** *Ps 145: 2-3, 4-5, 10-11*
   *Lk 16: 9-15 (On God and money)*

This collection of sayings stresses the importance of being honest with ourselves concerning our attachments to wealth. Significantly, these verses seem to be saying that our spiritual charity ought to be balanced by our generosity with material goods. The world might consider such a notion laughable, but God's priorities are not always the world's.

- Looking back over your reflection from yesterday, designate what you see to be the top three priorities in your life (consider time, rationale, etc.). Now take out another sheet of paper and, using the same three column headings, write in activities, time frames, and motives you would like your life to eventually reflect. How different is your second life sketch from the first? Why?

- Resolve to do something today to begin to bring your life more in line with where you want to go.

# Thirty-second
# Week in Ordinary Time

**Monday:** *Ps 139: 1-10*
   *Lk 17: 1-6 (The importance of good example)*

Because God reveals himself to us through human behavior, those of us committed to following Jesus Christ should be especially careful so as not to scandalize the innocent and the ignorant. It is therefore our duty to confront one another when we veer away from a life of love.

- "He who cannot forgive breaks the bridge over which he himself must pass," wrote George Herbert. How does withholding forgiveness hurt you?

- Is there a friend or loved one whose alcohol and/or drug use concerns you? If you are not sure as to how to confront this person, call a substance abuse counselor for help.

**Tuesday:** *Ps 34: 2-3, 16-19*
   *Lk 17: 7-10 (Christian duty)*

There are many times when we feel that our ministries of service should qualify us for extraordinary recognition. This temptation to impress others with our goodness should be countered by an admission that what we have done is not extraordinary, but is only our duty.

- What are some reasons why you fear reaching out? Resolve to work through at least one of these blocks to relationship.

- What are some of the ways you can affirm your loved ones for their love "duties" which you have taken for granted lately?

**Wednesday:** *Ps 82: 3-4, 6-7*
  *Lk 17: 11-19 (The attitude of gratitude)*

Life is such an incredible phenomenon! It may well be that our planet alone out of billions of galaxies and stars has proven to be hospitable to living organisms. Yet how sad it is that we do not properly appreciate the miracle that we are! It was gratitude that brought the Samaritan leper far more than health; it was to be his salvation.

- Do you believe it is a sin to take your life and creation for granted?

- Spend time thanking God for the gift of your life, your body and its functioning parts, your health, etc.

**Thursday:** *Ps 119: 89-91, 130, 135, 175*
  *Lk 17: 20-25 (The kingdom among us)*

An erroneous translation in the past had it that "the kingdom of God is within you." The more correct translation is, "The kingdom of God is among you." The implication of the new translation is that God's Spirit is most active in our relationships with one another.

- Where do you look for God? How can you tell when you are experiencing God?

- Spend some time with the passage, "The reign of God is already in your midst." Pray for the grace to be able to recognize God's presence through the day today.

**Friday:** *Ps 19: 2-5*
        *Lk 17: 26-37 (The end times)*

The life, death and resurrection of Jesus is a paradigm for the direction which history is to take. "He didn't teach us how to swim only to let us drown," sing the Imperials. This does not mean that Christians will be spared the experience of catastrophe, however. Our Lord, after all, had to pick up his own cross and face the powers of evil in this world.

- Do you believe that God would allow nuclear warfare to take place? Why? (Why not?)

- Do you, like St. Paul did 1,900 years ago, ever entertain the hope that perhaps Christ shall return before you die? Could this be a means of coping with your own fear of death?

**Saturday:** *Ps 105: 2-3, 36-37, 42-43*
        *Lk 18: 1-8 (Persist in prayer)*

"God is at least as good as a corrupt judge who, after all, gave in to the requests of a persistent widow," Jesus tells us in today's parable. It is when the going gets tough that our level of faith will show itself. If our faith is weak, we shall be overwhelmed by life's difficulties; if it is strong, we shall conquer the world.

- Do you find it difficult to pray when anxieties and suffering wear you down? How do you feel when you try to cope on your own?

- Ask God to give you the grace to work through a problem you've been struggling with lately. Believe that grace is yours, and resolve to work through this difficulty in truth and love.

# Thirty-third Week in Ordinary Time

**Monday:** *Ps 119: 53, 61, 134, 150, 155, 158*
   *Lk 18: 35-43 (The blind see!)*

Today we reflect on another example of the value of persistence. The blind man was not to be denied his opportunity to meet Jesus and request healing from him. Jesus rewarded his faith by granting his request.

- Jesus must have known very well what the blind man wanted from him, so why did he ask, "What do you want me to do for you?"

- Do you find it difficult to articulate your needs to others? If so, then how are they supposed to know how you need them to love you?

**Tuesday:** *Ps 3: 2-8*
   *Lk 19: 1-10 (Jesus and Zacchaeus)*

Tax collectors were men designated by Rome to extract from the Jews money owed Rome for services rendered by the government. They were despised by the Jews, for many Jews resented being governed by Rome and because it was common knowledge that tax collectors often extorted money for their own enrichment. Zacchaeus, the chief tax collector, must have been the focal point of much hatred, but this did not stop him from seeking out Jesus and subsequently reforming his life.

- Would you be willing to climb a tree to see Jesus Christ? Do you empathize with Zacchaeus' desire to be with Jesus?

- Resolve to invite to dinner someone with whom you have lost contact lately.

- Pray for the grace to desire a deeper relationship with Christ.

**Wednesday:** *Ps 17: 1, 5-6, 8, 15*
      *Lk 19: 11-28 (Parable of the pounds)*

Jesus may have based this story on an actual historical occurrence. When Herod the Great died, one of his sons, Archelaus, went to Rome to plead for his inheritance. A delegation of Jews dissuaded the emperor from appointing him king, but his inheritance was granted. Jesus builds into this incident a lesson concerning the wise use of our talents.

- "Since you are neither hot nor cold, but only lukewarm, I will spit you out of my mouth," said the risen Christ to the church in Laodicea (Rv 3: 16). What does this passage say to you?

- Have you been developing your talents and sharing yourself in challenging ways lately? How so?

**Thursday:** *Ps 50: 1-2, 5-6, 14-15*
      *Lk 9: 41-44 (Jesus weeps over Jerusalem)*

God wants so very much for us and we often

settle for so very little! This is what Jesus
lamented as he stood outside the gates of
Jerusalem, longing to share with the people of the
city the many graces at work through him. He
knew that he would be rejected, however, so he
wept for the suffering this would bring on his
people.

• What are some of the reasons why we settle for
  less than what God wants to give us? With
  which of these blocks to growth have you been
  struggling most lately?

• Are you satisfied with the promises made and
  goods delivered by proponents of the great
  American dream? Why? (Why not?)

• Pray for the grace to hunger for the things of
  God.

**Friday:** *1 Chr 29: 10-12*
     *Lk 19: 45-48 (Cleansing the Temple)*

In order to appreciate the zeal which moved
Jesus to chase out the traders in the Temple, we
must realize that the money-changers and sellers
of animals who had set up booths were victimiz-
ing the poor by offering them services at elevated
prices. It was this defilement of the people of God
in the name of his house which angered Jesus
most.

• How do you feel about your tax dollars going to
  the support of oppressive military regimes
  throughout the world?

- How do you feel about your Lord marching right into the midst of his enemies and confronting them?

- Pray for the grace to be courageous in your beliefs.

**Saturday:** *Ps 9: 2-4, 6, 16, 19*
*Lk 20: 27-40 (Confronting the Sadducees)*

Because the conservative Sadduccees did not believe in life after death, their notions of justice applied only to this life. When they presented their hypothetical case to Jesus in an effort to test him, Jesus promised that children of the resurrection would live with God forever. This promise should bring joy to us today.

- Do you ever fantasize about what heaven might be like? If a non-believer were to ask you why anyone should hope for heaven, what would you answer?

- "I believe that what we suffer in this life can never be compared to the glory, as yet unrevealed, which is waiting for us," wrote St. Paul (Rom 8: 18). Spend some time letting this hope buoy your spirit.

# Thirty-fourth Week in Ordinary Time

**Monday:** *Dn 3:52-56*
    *Lk 21: 1-4 (True giving)*

During this last week of the church's liturgical year, we will be considering some of the most important of all Christian truths. Today's short reading teaches us that when we give of our excess we have given very little of ourselves. Real giving involves risk—not only of financial resources, but of mental and spiritual as well.

- "The door into the kingdom of God opens from the inside out," goes a popular saying. "In giving you shall receive," St. Paul added. How do you understand these aphorisms? Have you experienced these truths working in your life recently? How can you work them today?

- Pray for the grace to recognize opportunities to give of yourself.


**Tuesday:** *Dn 3: 57-61*
    *Lk 21: 5-11 (The destruction of the Temple)*

The Temple which existed in Jerusalem at the time of Christ had taken decades of work to rebuild. Many believe that it rivaled the Temple built by Solomon in beauty and size. It was destroyed, however, by Vespasius' troops as they conclusively repressed Jewish insurrections in 70 A.D. In today's reading, Jesus warns us that the coming forth of God's kingdom will be accompanied by wars, destruction and suffering.

- Some philosophers maintain that either God can prevent evil but chooses not to, or else he cannot prevent evil at all (even though he might want to). What is your response to this statement?

- We live today in a climate of security based on a doctrine of nuclear deterrence. How does the peace of Christ keep you in the midst of this situation?

**Wednesday:** *Dn 3: 62-67*
  *Lk 21: 12-19 (Persevere through persecutions)*

Because Christians recognize that the status quo is never a full manifestation of the kingdom of God, we shall be persecuted by the idolaters of the status quo. Perseverance in love and truth shall win us a place in eternity, however, for our Lord has gone before us.

- Do you believe that heroism is dead? What are some "ordinary" examples of heroism with which you are familiar? Why have these people persevered in such noble ways?

- What are examples of heroic perseverance from your own life? How did you grow because of these experiences?

**Thursday:** *Dn 3: 68-74*
  *Lk 21: 20-28 (The second coming)*

The church has always believed that her risen

Lord would return. Just how, when and where this will come to pass we do not know for sure, despite the insistence of fundamentalist exegetes to the contrary. Jesus' teachings concerning his return come to us couched in the words of apocalyptic literature, which is highly symbolic and difficult to understand. It is enough for us to believe that history will not terminate in some catastrophic dead end; Christ shall one day be "all in all."

- What does the second coming mean to you?

- Do you believe that you shall be faced with the prospect of living through personal and/or national catastrophe before you die? If so, how do you propose to remain hopeful when these times come?

**Friday:** *Dn 3: 75-81*
    *Lk 21: 29-33 (Parable of the fig tree)*

Just as a fig tree shows signs when it is going to flower and bear fruit, so do ordinary circumstances give hints at what is to come. This does not mean that we ought to leave the future to itself, withdrawing from the world in fatalistic pessimism, however. Nothing could be farther from the Spirit of Jesus Christ.

- "Never put off something that can and should be done today," is a wise saying. Resolve to make a fresh start in whatever endeavors you have been avoiding lately.

- Spend some time with the passage, "Heaven and earth shall pass away, but my words will not pass." Invite the Holy Spirit to deepen your rootedness in God's love.

**Saturday:** *Dn 3: 82-87*
*Lk 21: 34-36 (Be watchful!)*

Jesus came that we might know God and that the power of sin in this world might be broken. His Spirit enables us to stand before God in peace and security, knowing that the kingdom which Jesus came to build shall eventually displace the kingdom of the world. That this vision might be realized, God invites us to strive constantly to grow in love, resisting indulgence and worldly cares. This struggle is a lifelong process.

- "Show me a thoroughly satisfied man, and I will show you a failure," wrote Thomas Edison. What did he mean by this?

- "Christianity is not a religion of ends, but one of means," wrote another great thinker. Do you believe that crooked means can ever produce straight ends? Why? (Why not?)

- Spend some time thanking God for the graces that have come to you through the church's liturgical ministry.